Contents

Helion & Company Limited
Unit 8 Amherst Business Centre
Budbrooke Road
Warwick
CV34 5WE
England
Tel. 01926 499 619
Email: info@helion.co.uk
Website: www.helion.co.uk
Twitter: @helionbooks
Visit our blog http://blog.helion.co.uk/

Text © Dr Dewald Venter 2020
Colour profiles © David Bocquelet 2020
Maps © Tom Cooper 2020
Photographs © as individually credited

Designed & typeset by Farr out Publications,
    Wokingham, Berkshire
Cover design by Paul Hewitt, Battlefield
    Design (www.battlefield-design.co.uk)

Printed for Helion & Co by Henry Ling Ltd.,
    Dorchester, Dorset

ISBN 978-1-913336-25-7

British Library Cataloguing-in-Publication
    Data
A catalogue record for this book is available
    from the British Library

We always welcome receiving book
proposals from prospective authors.

Note: In order to simplify the use of this book, all names, locations and geographic designations are as provided in *The Times World Atlas*, or other traditionally accepted major sources of reference, as of the time of described events. Correspondingly, the term 'Congo' designates the area of the former Belgian colony of the Congo Free State, granted independence as the Democratic Republic of the Congo in June 1960 and in use until 1971 when the country was renamed Republic of Zaire, which, in turn, reverted to Democratic Republic of the Congo in 1997, and which remains in use today. As such, Congo is not to be mistaken for the former French colony of Middle Congo (Moyen Congo), officially named the Republic of the Congo on its independence in August 1960, also known as Congo-Brazzaville.

Dedication

This book is dedicated to my grandfather, Wilhelmus Johannes de Beer (1929-1999), who fostered in me a love and appreciation for military heritage when I was four years old.

Abbreviations

2IC	Second in Command	FCP	Fire Control Post
61 Mech	61 Mechanised Battalion Group	FCS	Fire Control System
32 Bn	32 Battalion	FIB	Force Intervention Brigade
AAD	African Aerospace and Defence	FLIR	Forward Looking InfraRed
AC	Armoured Car	FO	Fire Orders
ADF	Allied Democratic Forces	gal	Gallon US
AGL	Automatic Grenade Launcher	GPS	Global Positioning System
AML	Auto Mitrailleuse Légère: Light Armoured Car	HE	High Explosive
AMV	Armoured Modular Vehicle	HE-I	High Explosive Incendiary
AP	Armour-Piercing	HEAT	High Explosive Anti-Tank
APC	Armoured Personnel Carrier	HEAT-T	High Explosive Anti-Tank Tracer
APCT	Armour-Piercing Core Tracer	HE-BB	High Explosive Base Bleed
APDS	Armour-Piercing Discarding Sabot	HE-FRAG	High Explosive Fragmentation
APFSDS	Armour-Piercing Fin Stabilised Discarding Sabot	HESH	High Explosive Squash Head
APFSDS-T	Armour-Piercing Fin Stabilised Discarding Sabot-Tracer	HE-T	High Explosive Tracer
		HIFF	High-Frequency Tank Fire Directing System
AP-I	Armour-Piercing Incendiary	HIT	High Impact Targets
APS	Active Protection System	HMG	Heavy Machine Gun
APU	Auxiliary Power Unit	hp	horsepower
ARMSCOR	Armaments Corporation of South Africa	hp/t	horsepower per ton
ARV	Armoured Recovery Vehicle	HQ	Headquarters
ATES	Artillery Target Engagement System	HVT	High-Value Targets
AU	African Union	IADSA	Industrial and Automotive Design South Africa
BAE	British Aerospace	ICV	Infantry Combat Vehicle
BLT	Bridge Laying Tank	IED	Improvised Explosive Device
BMG	Browning machine gun	IFCS	Integrated Fire Control System
C&C	Command and Control	IFV	Infantry Fighting Vehicle
CDU	Chemical Defence Unit	in	Inch
COIN	Counter Insurgency	IR	Infra Red
COP	Commander's Observation Platform	km	Kilometre
CRU	Chemical Research Unit	km/h	Kilometre per hour
CSI	Chief of Staff Intelligence	kW	Kilowatt
CSIR	Council for Scientific and Industrial Research	LCT	Light Combat Turret
CVED	Combat Vehicle Electric-Drive Demonstrator	LEW	Lyttleton Engineering Works
DENEL	South African armaments development and manufacturing company	LMG	Light Machine Gun
		LMS	Launcher Management System
DEXA	Defence Exhibition of South Africa	LMT	Land Mobility Technology
DLS	Denel Land Systems	MBT	Main Battle Tank
DRC	Democratic Republic of the Congo	MCS	Modular Charge System
DRU	Defence Research Unit	MDB	Mechanology Design Bureau
EADS	European Aeronautic, Defence and Space Company	MECHEM	MECHanical and ChEMical Research
EBR	Panhard Engin Blindé de Reconnaissance: Armoured Reconnaissance Vehicle	mi	Mile
		MICT	Modular Infantry Combat Turret
ER	Extended Range	Mk	Mark
ERA	Explosive Reactive Armour	mph	Miles per hour
ERFB	Extended Range Full Bore	MPCV	Mine-protected Combat Vehicle
ERF-BB	Extended Range Full Bore-Base Bleed	MPLA	Popular Movement for the Liberation of Angola
ESD	Electronics System Development	mrad	milliradian
EW	Electronic Warfare	MRAP	Mine-Resistant Ambush Protected
FAPLA	People's Armed Forces of Liberation of Angola	MRL	Multiple Rocket Launcher
ft	Feet	MRLS	Multiple Launch Rocket System
ft/s	Feet per second	ms	millisecond
FCM	Fighting Compartment Module	m/s	Meters per second

MTTD	Medium Turret Technology Demonstrator	**SATSC**	South African Technical Service Corps
MVMMDS	Vehicle Mounted Metal Detection System	**SPAAG**	Self-Propelled Anti-Aircraft Gun
NATO	North Atlantic Treaty Organization	**SPAAM**	Self-Propelled Anti-Aircraft Missile
NBC	Nuclear, Biological and Chemical	**SPADS**	Self-Propelled Air Defence System
NGICV	New Generation Infantry Combat Vehicle	**SRC**	Space Research Corporation
NGM	New Generation Missile	**SSB**	Special Service Battalion
OMC	Olifant Manufacturing Company	**SWA**	South West Africa
PLAN	People's Liberation Army of Namibia	**SWAPO**	South West Africa People's Organization
PMP	Pretoria Metal Pressing	**SWATF**	South West Africa Territorial Force
PPM	Pre Production Model	**SWB**	Short Wheel Base
QRF	Quick Reaction Force	**t**	ton
RHA	Rolled Homogenous Armour	**TTD**	Tank Technology Demonstrator
RPG	Rocket Propelled Grenades	**TV**	Television
SAAC	South African Armoured Corps	**UAE**	United Arab Emirates
SAAF	South African Air Force	**UCDD**	United Car and Diesel Distributors
SACS	SA Corps of Signals	**UDF**	Union Defence Force
SAD	Safety Arming Device	**UN**	United Nations
SADC	Southern African Development Community	**UNITA**	National Union for the Total Independence of Angola
SADF	South Africa Defence Force		
SAHV	South African High-Velocity Missile	**USSR**	Union of Soviet Socialist Republics
SAI	South African Infantry	**VAMIDS**	Vehicle Array Mine Detection System
SAMHS	South African Military Health Service	**VHF**	Very High Frequency
SAMIL	South African Military	**V-Lap**	Velocity-Enhanced Long-range Artillery Projectile
SANDF	South Africa National Defence Force	**WP-SMK**	White Phosphorus Smoke
SAP	South African Police	**WW2**	World War Two
SAPS	South African Police Service	**yd**	Yard
SAPHEI	Semi-Armour-Piercing-High-Explosive-Incendiary		

Acknowledgements

This book was written over four years and would not have been possible if it was not for the assistance of the individuals who designed, managed, tested and used the vehicles. Their first-hand knowledge and dedication resulted in ideas on paper evolving to become some of the finest military vehicles ever produced. Interviewing each gave me invaluable insight into the unique story of each vehicle.

Brigadier General (retd) Tony Savides, one of the fathers of the Ratel and former SA Army project director who oversaw the design and production of several of the vehicles in this book. Always willing to assist, clarify and point me in the right direction, together with several other key authors who recently completed their two-volume book on the Ratel ICV. A winner for sure and exciting future read. Former General Officer Commanding SA Army Armour Formation, Brigadier General (retd) André Retief who permitted my research at the SA Army School of Armour, 1 SSB and SA Armour Museum. His appreciation for military history contributed to making this book possible. Desmond Gardner, former Director of OMC Engineering for his technical guidance and support. Always willing to lend a hand.

Every interviewee whom I met in person, over the phone, via email or social media and told their story. The photo contributors for sharing memories, they add depth to what would otherwise be just pages with detailed text. To the contributors of the soldiers' stories, thank you for diving deep and sharing your experiences.

David Bocquelet, chief editor at Tank Encyclopaedia for allowing me to become part of his team and Stan Lucian for all the 11th-hour proofreading.

Tom Cooper and the team from the @War Series for their enthusiasm to publish my work.

My wife Carina for her support, encouragement and understanding for my writing addiction on military matters. My daughter Ciska who at this stage is too young to understand but always shows enthusiasm when daddy starts talking about his visit to the army. My parents and parents-in-law for their support.

Lastly, to the next generation of authors. I hope this book inspires your imagination and love for military heritage and encourages you to visit and support your local military museums.

Author's notes

Writing a military book has always been a dream and has since become a passion. This passion is also reflected in my academic research into military heritage. Much of what is captured in this book consists of information I could not find in other publications on South African armoured vehicles; hence I set out to gather what was missing. Each journey has its challenges. Ensuring accuracy, gaining access and finding time were the most challenging factors.

Accurate historical information in a printed format on South African military vehicles is hard to come by, given the secrecy that surrounded their initial development. The official files on the majority of the vehicles are still secret and will only be declassified and available for public access around 2025. To ensure accuracy, I approached the people who planned, produced and worked on the vehicles. Many of the companies who were responsible for the vehicles' research and development are no longer in existence, have merged with other companies, or have completely changed. The staff are now working elsewhere, retired or no longer alive. Finding the players of these key roles was not easy but proved invaluable for getting the facts straight for the record and disproving inaccurate information found on the internet and elsewhere. With the support and help of the South African Army Armour Formation, I was allowed access to their vehicles and archives for research purposes as well as interviewing the soldiers who operate most of the vehicles found in the book. Social media proved to be a blessing as various South African military heritage groups graciously allowed me to join their ranks to source contacts and information. Interviews with military veterans also formed a core component of the book's content, as their knowledge and first-hand experience is invaluable.

As a full-time university academic, researcher, husband and father, time was a scarce commodity. Writing mostly took place during holidays, weekends and late weeknights over the course of four years.

For ease and convenience, each chapter focuses on a single armoured vehicle. Each vehicle's development history is unpacked, followed by its design characteristics which entail mobility, endurance and logistics, vehicle layout, main armament, fire control system and protection. I then look at variants of the vehicle, the combat actions it took part in and lastly a conclusion is presented. Several veterans submitted their accounts of experience with the vehicle they used and for which I am very grateful. For quick reference, an illustrated side profile of each vehicle is provided with a summary of the vehicle's specifications.

South Africans can be proud of what was accomplished by our defence industry during the Cold War when the challenges were many, but the talent was plentiful. The English proverb "necessity is the mother of invention" has never been more valid than it was for South Africa during that time. South Africa still produces some of the most remarkable armoured vehicles in the world.

Dr Dewald Venter

Foreword

Dr Dewald Venter is an armoured vehicle enthusiast with a professional approach and dedication to the subject. He has been of great help to our team and me during the editing phase of the book on the Ratel ICV, which was published in 2020.

There have been several publications over the years covering the range of armoured vehicles developed for the SADF, its predecessor the UDF and its successor, the SANDF, but in this latest publication, Dewald has chosen not to cover the whole spectrum, nor to concentrate (as the Ratel book does) on a single-vehicle system. Instead, he has selected those vehicle systems which, to a degree, have become icons, primarily for the role they played in the Border War, but also, in some cases, for the role they might have played had they been available at the time. There are thus ten vehicle systems with a triple dose of the Olifant MBT.

The result is a veritable "Who's Who" of the SA armoured vehicle systems in a concise yet detailed form for the enthusiast and the historian, and for those who saw combat in some of the vehicles. The subject has been widely and deeply researched from archival documents to personal interviews and, while cognisant of some differences in fact and opinion, Dewald has compiled a worthy and credible publication. There, will, of course, be different views and even criticism on some detail of his entries, mostly well-intended

but, as is sometimes the case, also from those who would rather seek fault than attempt a work such as this themselves.

Technically, in SADF parlance anyway, mine-protected vehicles such as the Buffel, Casspir and the Kwêvoël-based Bateleur were not classified nor managed as armoured vehicles ("A-vehicles") but rather as B-vehicles that were adapted from or designed on the components and aggregates of soft-skinned vehicles – but this matters not, other than "for the record".

Having been involved in SA Army projects for over a decade between 1975 and 1990 (with two short breaks), I was privileged to be part of the development of some of the vehicle systems covered in this publication or, at least, to have seen them come to fruition in my term as Director Projects at Army HQ. I was not destined to see combat to any great extent and while saluting those who were, I also salute the individuals, organisations and companies that were involved in the conceptualisation, design, development, production and support of the phenomenal vehicle systems that were produced before, during and after the Border War, and which are featured in Dewald Venter's book.

Thank you, Dewald, for your dedication and professionalism and for a great publication!

Brigadier General (Retd) Tony Savides

Framing South African armour development

A battlespace refers to the environment, features and circumstances in the operational area that has an impact on friendly and enemy military forces' (land, air, sea) ability to complete their mission. These may include terrain and its effect on communication, infrastructure, weather conditions, civilian population and

intelligence. The southern African battlespace, as with any, presents its own unique challenges.

According to de Vries in his 2013 book, the African battlespace consists of challenging terrain and environmental challenges. These include poor road infrastructure, limited access routes, long travel distances, difficult and heavy brushed terrain to negotiate and minimal resources for sustainment. Such challenges make travelling, manoeuvring, fighting and logistical supply extremely difficult. Additionally de Vries states that there was always more than one avenue of approach to choose from; wide open spaces through which to infiltrate and vast cover to hide in from the ground and air detection.

Camp and Heitman, writing in 2014, state that there were several reasons why the SADF favoured wheeled designs above tracked. For the southern African battlespace wheeled vehicles offer a greater logistical and strategic advantage as they offer higher flexibility for fast-moving operations, are between 40-60% cheaper, have a 300% longer service life, use 60% less fuel and maintenance intervals are between 200-300% longer. Additionally, wheeled vehicles require a smaller power pack to achieve the same performance as a similar tracked vehicle. Tracked vehicles are much more susceptible to landmine blasts which de-track and immobilises them. In contrast, some wheeled configurations, such as the Rooikat and Ratel, can remain mobile after striking a mine. Making use of wheels instead of tracks allowed for better operational mobility over long distances and favoured the manoeuvre warfare practised by the SADF as opposed to FAPLA and Cuban forces who followed position warfare doctrine.

South African vehicles were explicitly designed and hardened to cope with these conditions which allowed them to *bundu bash*. The term will be used often in the book and refers to the process or action of driving through – instead of around – small trees and dense vegetation. The ability of South African armoured vehicles to literally break the bush would become a standard feature and allowed them to avoid landmine-riddled dirt roads, and make use of the indirect approach through the bush to their designated objectives, often catching FAPLA and Cuban forces off guard.

For readers who want a more in-depth read on armoured vehicle application in Africa, I would suggest *Mobile Warfare for Africa: On the Successful Conduct of Wars in Africa and Beyond – Lessons Learned from the South African Border War*, by de Vries, Burger and Steencamp, also published by Helion and Company (see bibliography for full details).

1

Eland Armoured Car

THE AFRICAN ANTELOPE

The Eland armoured car, more affectionately known by its nickname "Noddy Car", with reference to the famous Enid Blyton character, takes its Afrikaans name from the African Eland, the largest antelope in the world. Similar to its namesake, the Eland evolved to adapt to the harsh Southern African environment.

DEVELOPMENT

Up until the late 1950s, the UDF – which would become the SADF – made use of the British-built Ferret armoured car. A subsequent macro environmental study in the early 1960s showed that the most likely conflict South Africa would become involved in would take the form of expeditionary missions and counter insurgencies for which the Ferret was not suited. This shortcoming necessitated the acquisition of a more-modern, lightweight, lightly armoured, well-armed, long-range reconnaissance vehicle. Initially, three armoured cars were considered, namely the Saladin, the Panhard EBR, and the Panhard AML. Ultimately the four-wheeled AML was deemed the most appropriate to fulfil the desired role South Africa had in mind.

The initial testing of the AML 60 with its 60mm Brandt Mle CM60A1 breech-loading gun-mortar showed that the weapon was lacking in firepower and South Africa requested a heavier weapon. This led Panhard to design a new turret which would accommodate a DEFA 90mm low-pressure quick-firing gun. South Africa purchased 100 AMLs as well as additional turrets, engines, and parts for the assembly of 800 more armoured cars. The manufacturing of the AML 60 and 90 (rebranded as the Eland 60 and 90) would become one of South Africa's most ambitious weapon manufacturing programs, post-Second World War. Production by the South African industrial firm Sandrock-Austral of the AML 60 and 90 subsequently began in 1961 with the first batch entering service trials in 1962 as the Eland Mk1. In essence, they were still French AML 60 and 90s. These armoured cars included 40% local content with the majority of parts being purchased from Panhard.

South Africa acquired the licenses to produce the vehicle hull and turret independently from Panhard in 1964. The turret was manufactured by Austral Engineering in Wadeville and the hull by

A troop of Eland 90 Mk7 armoured cars at Grootfontein in the mid-1980s. (E. Prinsloo)

Sandock Austral in Boksburg and Durban. What followed was a series of improvements which would make the armoured car more suited for the African terrain. The Eland Mk2 featured an improved steering system and brakes, of which 56 were delivered, while the Eland Mk3 saw the installation of a new custom-built fuel system. The Eland Mk4 incorporated two more modifications which included the replacement of the electric clutch with a more reliable conventional model and the movement of the FCS from the gunner's feet to the turret hand crank. Additional smaller improvements were made, such as replacing the chain holding the fuel cap with a cable – which made less noise. By 1967, the South African manufactured armoured cars only resembled their French counterparts externally while making use of 66% South African produced parts.

From 1972, 356 Eland Mk5 armoured cars would be built. They featured a new General Motors 2.5l, water-cooled four-cylinder inline petrol engine mounted on rails to facilitate quicker replacement in the field (just 40 minutes) and reduce maintenance. Additional improvements included new communication equipment, spring shock absorbers, wheels, and run-flat tyres.

In 1975 the Mk6 upgrade brought 1,016 (all the previously produced Eland Marks) up to the Mk5 standard. The final version of the Eland, the Mk7, was put into production in 1979 and featured a new raised commander's cupola derived from the Ratel ICV, moving of the headlamps from the lower glacis to a raised position, new power brakes, improved transmission, and a lengthened frontal section to make the driver's station more comfortable for the taller than average South African soldier.

The Eland 60 and 90 became the standard armoured car for the SADF's armoured car regiments and served in a reconnaissance role when assigned to the tank regiment. The SADF deployed the Eland with the permanent forces at the SA Army School of Armour, 1 South African Tank Regiment and 2 South African Tank Regiment. With the reserve forces, the Eland was used by Natal Mounted Rifles, Umvoti Mounted Rifles, Regiment Oranje Rivier (Cape Town), Regiment Mooirivier (Potchefstroom), Regiment Molopo (Potchefstroom), Light Horse, President Steyn, Prince Alfred Guards, 2 Armoured Car Regiment, 8th Division (Durban), Head of the Armed Forces Mobile Reserve and Armed Forces Mobile Centre (formerly 7th Division). In South West Africa the Eland was used by the South West Territorial and 2 SAI (Walvisbay).

The Eland was removed from frontline service in the late 1980s when its indigenously produced replacement, the Rooikat 76 armoured car, began to enter service. The Eland was officially retired from SANDF service in 1994. In South Africa, the Eland can be found at most military bases as gate guards and several pairs, in working condition, are preserved at military museums including the SA Armour Museum in Bloemfontein. Several Elands have also found their way into the hands of private collectors and foreign museums.

By the end of its production, more than 1,600 vehicles had been built. The Eland family of armoured cars, which also includes a 20mm quick-firing cannon armed version, are still in service with foreign armies which include, Benin, Burkina Faso, Chad, Gabon, Ivory Coast, Malawi, Morocco, Sahrawi Arab Democratic Republic, Senegal, Uganda, and Zimbabwe.

DESIGN FEATURES

The Eland saw continued design improvements over the original AML throughout its production, making it more capable in the African battlespace. In line with its role as a lightweight, heavily armed reconnaissance vehicle, the Eland could pack a decisive punch when needed, making it a versatile weapon platform for its time. The following sections will specifically cover the Mk7 variant unless otherwise stated.

Mobility

The Southern African battlespace favoured the Eland's permanent 4×4 configuration. It was fitted with four split rims 12:00x16 track grip tubeless run-flat Dunlop tyres – designed to resist the effects of deflation when punctured – which resulted in more reliability and mobility. The suspension consisted of fully independent trailing arm type, single spiral coil springs and double action hydraulic shock absorbers on each wheel station.

The Eland had a manual transmission with a constant mesh gearbox. The gear selection range consisted of both low and high range, with six forward, one neutral, and one reverse gear. For off-road use, the two low gears, one top gear, and reverse were used. When in low range, the standard drive's four ratios of the high range were used for the three upper gears of the range, four to six. The high range was used for road driving and had three low gears and overdrive. The Eland was not amphibious, but it could ford 82cm (32.3in) of water with preparation (fitting plugs in the floor).

The Eland was powered by a General Motors 4-cylinder 2.5l petrol engine, which could produce 87hp (65kW) at 4,600rpm and provide a 16.4hp/t power to weight ratio for the Eland 60 and 14.5hp/t for the Eland 90. The maximum road speed was 90km/h (56mph) with a recommended safe cruising speed of 80km/h (50mph). Over terrain, it could achieve 30km/h (18.6mph).

The Eland could cross a 50cm (19.7in) wide ditch at a crawl and climb a 51% gradient. On the front of the vehicle were

Eland 90 Mk7 – South African National Museum of Military History. (S. Tegner)

two ditch-crossing channels which allowed the Eland to cross ditches up to 3.2m (10.5ft) wide when using four channels. The vehicle was equipped with fully independent active trailing arms, coil springs, and shock-absorbers. Steering was via a steering wheel with rack and pinion assisted power gearbox and the mechanical power steering box improved the driver's steering ability on rough terrain. Steering was controlled with the front two wheels and foot pedals for acceleration and braking. The Eland 90 had a ground clearance of 380mm (15in) and the Eland 60 400mm (15.8in) which in combination with only four wheels sometimes resulted in it becoming stuck when travelling off-road, which was obviously far from ideal.

Eland 60 Mk7 – SA Armour Museum. (D. Venter)

Endurance and logistics

The fuel capacity of the Eland was 142ℓ (37.5gal) which allowed it to travel 450km (280mi) on-road, 240km (149mi) off-road and 120km (74.5mi) over-sand.

The Eland 90 and 60 were equipped with two 7.62mm BMGs, one mounted co-axially and the other on top of the turret structure, above the commander's station, for close protection from ground threats. The Eland 90 carried 3,800 rounds for the machine guns, and the Eland 60, 2,400 rounds. It should be noted that creative stacking would allow for more machine gun rounds to be carried. The co-axial machine gun was mounted on the left side of the main armament in both variants.

Eland 90 Mk7 – Driver's station – SA Armour Museum. (D. Venter)

At the rear right-hand side of the turret, behind the gunner were a B-56 long-range and B-26 short-range radio set for tactical communication which allowed for reliable command and control, enhancing the armoured car's force multiplier effect on the battlefield. This communication, combined with well-trained crews, resulted in co-ordinated (but nail-biting) attacks on T-54/55 MBTs during Operation Askari.

The Eland Mk7 received a much-needed storage bin at the rear of the turret. Pre-Mk7 Elands did not have a built-in drinking water tank and crews subsequently had to carry water in a 20ℓ (5.2gal) jerry can attached to the outside of the driver's left entry door with a bracket. Crews improvised and kept non-drinking water in used

ammunition boxes and spent main gun casings on the outside of the hull. The Mk7 features a built-in 40ℓ (10.5gal) drinking water tank installed at the rear of the vehicle from where the crew could access it via a brass push tap.

Vehicle layout

The Eland carried a standard complement of three crew members, consisting of the commander, gunner, and driver.

The commander's station was located on the left side of the turret while the gunner was seated on the right. The turret was fitted with two L794D periscopes for observation while closed down. A raised vision cupola was fitted in the turret roof over the commander's position which gave him a 360-degree view while inside the turret.

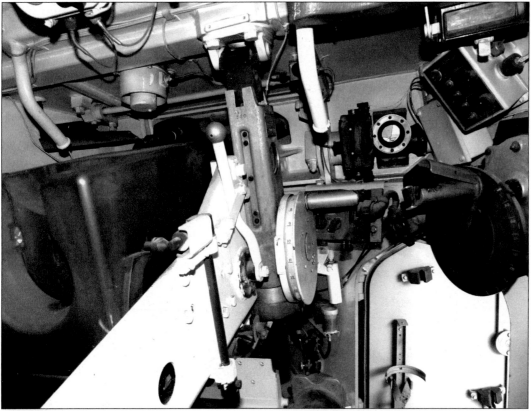

Eland 90 Mk7- From the gunners' seat looking forward. The gun breech block is on the left, turret hand crank and firing switches are on the far right and the vertical aim drive is on the right of the breech block. (S. Tegner)

Eland 90 Mk7 – From the gunners' seat facing backwards to the rear of the turret. The additional six-round first stage ammunition rack can be seen on the left of the photo. The radio equipment would be located in between the ammunition racks. (S. Tegner)

the forward and rear wheel. Of interest is the pistol port situated on the front left side of the hull through which the commander could shoot if necessary.

The driver's station was situated in the front centre of the hull and was accessible through the side entry doors as mentioned above or a single-piece hatch which opened to the right above the driver's station. The driver's station had limited adjustability making it difficult for tall drivers to operate. The single-piece hatch contained three integrated periscopes for enhanced vision and situational awareness. The central periscope could be replaced with a passive night driving episcope manufactured by Eloptro, allowing full day/night capability.

Main armament

The Eland 90 was armed with the GIAT 90mm F1 gun which was designated the GT-2 in South Africa and manufactured by Denel Land Systems. For combat, it could fire low-velocity HE, HEAT-T, WP-SMK, and canister rounds. The HE was accurate up to 2.2km (1.36mi) and the HEAT-T 1.2km (0.75mi) and could penetrate up to 320mm (12.6in) of RHA at zero degrees and 150mm (5.9in) at a 60-degree angle. The penetration and after armour effect of the HEAT-T round was devastating against the T34/85 that the South Africans faced in the early stages of the South African Border War. When the T-54/55 entered the conflict, South African Eland 90 crews had to make full use of their vehicles' small size and speed to flank

The commander could direct the gunner onto a target making use of a line sight. The gunner made use of an M494 sighting scope which provided x6 magnification for laying the main armament.

Entry and exit for the commander and gunner of an Eland 90 were via separate single-piece hatch covers for each which opened to the rear, whilst the Eland 60 had one elongated hatch for both commander and gunner which also opened to the back. In case of emergency, the gunner and commander could escape through the driver's entry doors located on either side of the hull in-between

them. Multiple shots from the Eland 90 were necessary to disable and destroy the new tanks.

The HE round weighed in at 5.27kg (11.6lb) and was very effective against lightly armoured vehicles, trenches, and bunkers. To control the recoil of the main gun, a single-cylinder with permanent stress spring and a hydropneumatic recuperator was used to return the main gun to its original position after firing. A well-trained crew could fire the main gun either when static or at a short halt every 8-10 seconds. The turret could be rotated a full 360 degrees in under 25 seconds although the standard practice was not to exceed 90 degrees left or right of centre. The main gun could elevate from -8 degrees to +15 degrees. Due to its small size, the Eland 90 carried 29 main gun rounds. A total of 16 were stored in the rear of the turret, five each behind the vehicle commander's and gunner's seat respectively and a further three at the bottom right of the turret basket.

The Eland 60 retained the original AML 60 turret and made use of the South African manufactured 60mm M2 breech-loading gun-mortar. It could fire a 1.72kg (3.70lb) bomb at 200m/s (656ft) up to 300m (328yd) in the direct-fire role and 2km (1.24mi) in the indirect-fire role. A total of 56 bombs were carried which consisted of a combination of bombs and illumination rounds. The main armament could elevate from -11 to +75 degrees. The rate of fire was on average, 6-8 bombs a minute. It was primarily used in the counter-insurgency and convoy protection role as its main gun was devastatingly effective against infantry. It mainly served in SWA's (Namibia's) northern operational areas.

Fire control system

The gunner made use of an Eloptro x6 gunner's day sight. Laying the Eland 90's gun was accomplished via hand-crank while sighting by the gunner was via a telescopic sight linked to the main gun. The Eland 90's main gun was not stabilised due to the lack of a turret drive and this required exceptionally skilled Eland 90 crews who had to work in concert to engage enemy targets as quickly as possible, minimising their exposure to targets and then withdrawing before they could be shot at in return.

Protection

The Eland consisted of a welded steel-plated hull between 8-12mm (0.3 and 0.47in) thick providing all-round protection against rifle fire, grenades, and medium artillery velocity fragments. It was, however, susceptible to anything bigger than 12.7mm in calibre. Two banks each of two electrically operated 81mm smoke grenade launchers were located on the rear left and right side of the turret and were used for self-screening in an emergency. There were two tubes to the rear of the left smoke grenade launchers which were often confused with the former but were however used to house the main gun cleaning brush. The frontal headlamps were under armoured covers and located on the frontal glacis where they were raised to protect against damage when driving through the bush. Due to its small size, the vehicle was never equipped with a fire suppression system but crews had at their disposal several hand-held fire extinguishers, one on the front right exterior of the vehicle, above the right wheel, and one inside the crew compartment.

Eland 90 Mk7 – The difference between the Eland 90 Mk7 and AML 90 is clearly seen with the engine compartment, rear left and right of hull having a different design. The additional rear turret stowage bin can also be seen. (South African National Museum of Military History. S. Tegner)

ELAND FAMILY

Eland 20

In 1971 the SAAC placed the requirement for an Eland fitted with a 20mm main gun. An Eland 60 named *Vuilbaard* (Dirty beard) was fitted with a Hispano-Suiza 20mm as a feasibility test. The results were not satisfactory, and in early 1972 this was repeated by installing an F2 20mm (imported for the Ratel 20 ICV project) in a turret. Both turrets were tested in a shoot-off against one another, and the F2 came out on top. By that time, however, the SAAC had dropped the requirement and focused on the Eland 60 and 90. The Eland 20 made use of exactly the same turret as used on the Ratel 20. The 20mm F2 cannon could fire in single, single-automatic (80 rounds per minute) and automatic (750 rounds per minute) modes and had the added advantage of being dual fed which meant that the gunner could switch between HE and AP with the flick of a switch. It also retained the co-axial 7.62mm machine gun and could also mount an additional 7.62mm machine gun on its roof. Ultimately Morocco purchased 30 Eland 20 armoured cars around 1980-1981.

Eland ENTAC

During the late 1960s, the SADF conducted a war game simulating an invasion of SWA. One of the shortcomings identified was that the Eland 90 lacked the punch necessary to engage potential enemy MBTs. To overcome this shortcoming, two external rails were added to the Eland turret, each of which could accommodate an ENTAC wire-guided anti-tank missile. The plan never went past the testing phase.

Eland 90TD

With the Eland phasing out of SADF service Reumech OMC saw an opportunity to further improve the Eland Mk7 with the aim of achieving foreign sales. The Eland 90TD was fitted with a turbocharged, water-cooled four-cylinder diesel engine which produced similar hp to the petrol engine but was much more reliable and much less flammable. It's unclear if any Eland TD variants were

Eland 90 Mk7 – The crew at work freeing their vehicle, after it bogged down in a flooded shona (flood plain) during the annual rainy season in Owamboland SWA. (N.B.C van der Walt)

manning roadblocks, and conducting search and destroy operations in SWA. Eland 90s were also used as training vehicles for Ratel 90 crews.

The last significant use of the Eland took place at the height of the South African Border War during Operation Moduler. On 5 October 1987, Eland 90s supported by infantry equipped with anti-tank weaponry set up an ambush north of Ongiva. The ambush was a success, and the SADF forces ambushed and destroyed a FAPLA motorised contingent consisting of BTR-60 and BTR-40 APCs, and truck-mounted infantry as they advanced to Ongiva.

CONCLUSION

With the conclusion of the South African Border War in 1989 and subsequent peace, defence spending was drastically cut. Having been succeeded by the Rooikat 76, the Eland's end was on the horizon. The SADF for a brief period considered keeping at least one squadron of Elands active should the need arise for an air-portable armour capability. This was, however, quickly set aside as the need for deploying forces outside the border was very remote, and due to the continued pressure to reduce the quantity of older equipment. Subsequently, the new SANDF retired the Eland from service in 1994. This decision would be proven wrong as the SANDF would deploy across Africa as part of UN peacekeeping missions. The Eland is still in service with various African countries.

ever sold. The company Mechanology also upgraded AML 90s for Mali with a diesel engine and day/night fighting capability.

OPERATIONAL HISTORY

The Eland served with distinction in the SADF for nearly three decades, the majority of the time spent during the South African Border War. As predicted, the conflict took the form of a cross border insurgency and the Eland was subsequently deployed to the northern part of SWA in 1969 to counter the threat. PLAN insurgents then began a campaign of mine warfare to disrupt the South African transportation and logistics network which lasted for two decades. Elands were tasked with escorting convoys, and it soon became apparent that they had difficulty moving off-road and were vulnerable to landmines. This resulted in South Africa's drive to develop mine-resistant vehicles such as the Buffel APC and Casspir APC, which would take over the patrolling and counter-insurgency roles. This need for mine-resistant vehicles led South Africa to become a world leader in the field out of necessity.

The Eland 90 played a valuable role as a reconnaissance, anti-armour, and fire support platform during the South African Border War. It was involved in various SADF operations including Savannah, Reindeer, Sceptic, Protea and Askari. It was during Operation Askari that the limitations of the Eland 90s were reached. The introduction by FAPLA of T54/55 MBTs stretched the Eland 90 crews to their limit as the MBTs required multiple hits from several armoured cars to set them ablaze. The limited number of main gun rounds carried made such engagements problematic and hastened the fatigue of the main gun's recoil system. Additionally, the Eland 90 could not match the off-road performance of the Ratel 90. A review panel post-Operation Askari noted the advancing age of the Eland 90 among the shortcomings of the operation. The subsequent primary anti-armour role was passed on to the Ratel 90 which made use of the same turrets as the Eland 90 but who's height advantage gave it better situational awareness in addition to its better overall performance. The Eland 60 and 90 were again relegated to escorting convoys, conducting joint patrols, guarding strategic installations,

A soldier's story – Spikkels' Eland driver

The following event took place during the 1983 Operations area near Etosha Game Reserve during a COIN patrol to prevent SWAPO infiltration.

The chaplain's nickname was "Spikkels". He was Troop Sergeant with one of the P car Troops! During his movement along the Game Park border, his driver made many significant judgment errors! The local Ovambos cut off the young trees about a foot from the ground and used the stems for poles when building their villages. The drivers had to be very careful, for these low protruding stems can easily rip off the Eland's steering arm! Needless to say, Spikkels' driver didn't look carefully enough and drove over one of these low stems, and the Eland's steering arm was ripped off. Spikkels told the driver to get out!

Spikkels calls a medic upfront and commandeers a white patch, then goes about fixing Fiji Meibo Binoculars with a bandage around the driver's head, which he had to walk around with all day.

Spikkels' reaction to the somewhat confused driver was "*now I hope you never drive over low protruding stems again*"!

Senior Warrant Officer (retd) S. Marais

A soldier's story – Eland 90

Firing the Eland 90's main gun was an experience for every crew member. You, as a recruit or a rookie, did not have the faintest idea what that main gun could do, despite previous exercises attended where we were spectators. The 90mm gun punch and kickback was immense. The air displacement when the main gun fired felt like a hard slap on your face. Some guys' noses started bleeding from the pressure displacement. As the training progressed, we became used to it and enjoyed it more and more. The type of ammunition we used [were] an exercise round (blue), a HE (olive green) and finally a canister round, which

Eland 90 Mk6 – Outside Grootfontein in 1977. (N. Bowden)

contained one thousand lead balls. This canister round could do a lot of damage to soft-skin vehicles at short distances of up to 400m (437yd). The canister round was also sometimes used where the bushes were very dense, and an open lap pocket or lane could then be shot with such round.

I had three operations in Angola during three border visits, the first of which was in 1987. Oshikati, Sector 10, during which General Swarthand Serfontein was our sector commander. Commander Jan Boland Du Toit was the armoured base commander. Each was a unique experience. The furthest we travelled into Angola was in 1989, near Cuvelai, where we were part of the reinforced group attack who would attack Cuvelai until we were unexpectedly given the command to return to Oshikati. We were all surprised, and in a way relieved too. I believe you know the reasons and the politics behind the decision, which I only found out years after the war.

A final anecdote to conclude. My colleague and friend troop commander of the time, Lieutenant Kat Snyman (Little Nephew of Armor Samejoor Kat Snyman), was part of a reinforced fighting group under the command of Commandant Jan Malan and Commandant Stoof du Doit. We were deployed in the vicinity of Mupa, Evali and Zngongo, with the aim of carrying out fox hunting (COIN) operations. 32 Battalion and a few UK men were also deployed with us. Lt Snyman was instructed to set up an ambush after receiving information from 32 Battalion that a large convoy of FAPLA would pass through the route along which we were deployed. The convoy consisted of BMPs, BRDMs, and Air Defence 23mm cannons mounted on their trailer chassis as well as various personnel carrier and logistics trucks.

Kat moved into position during the early evening hours with his reinforced Eland 90 troop, integrated with a platoon of infantry, about 50m (77yd) from the road. They camouflaged and waited. When the first FAPLA convoy vehicle was in line just before the last armoured car in line, they opened fire. The front vehicle in convoy was shot out, and it blocked the rest of the convoy. The convoy was struck, and the Eland 90 troop and infantry did great damage during the ensuing firefight. After the worst was over, Kat's Eland 90 group immediately returned to their hidden camp

area. Upon arrival, Kat gave feedback to the commanders, and everyone was pleased about the successful ambush, with no losses on our part. The only bad news was that while preparing for the ambush, one of the infantry Buffel drivers parked his APC against a tree. When Kat's group began to withdraw, the driver could not move the Buffel quickly enough, and a hasty decision was made to transfer the equipment and weapons to other vehicles and withdraw. At the time, some of the BRDMs and BTRs that had not been shot started a search for Kat's group, who got away just in time. A troop sergeant, Sergeant Greef, was called in shortly after the feedback session and was instructed to fetch the Buffel and bring it back.

It was already after 01:00 in the morning when we were preparing to depart. With our arrival on the scene, we very carefully and slowly began to look for the Buffel in the area, but there was no sign of it. My troop and I saw the damage that was done, and many of the vehicles that had been fired upon were still burning fiercely. Ammunition inside the vehicles exploded during our search. Some of the lighter vehicles that were shot out were moved to approximately 3m (9.8ft) from the road due to the impact of the 90mm gun at close range. I reported back that the Buffel tracks near the tree could be clearly seen, but FAPLA had already removed it. On our return, we avoided our own tracks as FAPLA would certainly have planted landmine[s] on our route. We returned during the early morning hours to report the bad news. The commanders were sceptical at first, which was short-lived. At 11:00, the SA Air Force flew over the area and reported seeing a convoy heading back to Luanda. The Buffel was leading the convoy. The pilot tried to shoot the Buffel but was unsuccessful. Today that same Buffel stands in Luanda's war museum, which I visited myself years later.

Major (retd) D. van Aswegen

2

Buffel Mine Protected Vehicle

THE AFRICAN BUFFALO

The Buffel was the second mass-produced open-topped APC with a V-shaped hull, after the Hippo MPV of which more than 200 were built. The Buffel would become a staple vehicle for SADF motorised units in SWA where it was primarily used for patrol duties along the Caprivi Strip on the northern border with Angola, and for COIN operations. It was designed to be mobile and provide protection against anti-tank mines, small arms fire, and shrapnel. The Buffel was phased out of frontline SADF service during the late 1980s and was relegated to internal security use until it was replaced by the Mamba APC in 1995.

DEVELOPMENT

From 1973 onwards, there was a sharp increase in landmine usage by SWAPO, which was fighting an insurgency war against South Africa for the independence of SWA. SWAPO operated from bases inside Angola and mostly crossed the SWA border through the Caprivi Strip. The SADF at that time had no dedicated mass-produced border-patrol MPV/APC which could protect the occupants against anti-personnel and anti-tank landmines. The 'soft skin' Unimog's rear passenger compartment was fitted with improvised sandbags and conveyor belt strips, which offered some protection to the occupants against landmine blasts.

The SADF had purchased 200 Mercedes-Benz Unimog S (416.162) trucks during the 1960s, which featured OM352 6-cylinder water-cooled diesel engines. Given the increased threat from landmines, the DRU was tasked by the SADF with improving the crew survivability of its Unimog fleet. The improvement to the Unimog chassis led to the production of the *"Bosvark"* (Bushpig) vehicle at 61 Base Workshop Unit in Pretoria.

The Bosvark featured a V-shaped rear tub made from mild steel which replaced the standard seat section, whilst the driver's frontal cab section received Barber mine-blast deflection plates. These improvements, while successful, did not protect the occupants from small arms fire. A total of 56 vehicles were produced and used successfully during Operation Savannah, the first major military incursion into Angola by the SADF in support of the UNITA, which was fighting a war against the Cuban and Soviet-backed MPLA and the Angolan conventional army, the FAPLA, for control of Angola.

Post-Operation Savannah, the SADF conducted a needs assessment of their entire fleet. This would later lead to the SAMIL range of vehicles. Messrs UCDD, who upgraded the Unimogs, came to hear of the new developments and feared a loss in future military contracts. Thus, they set out to further develop the Bosvark into a dedicated MPV which would function as an APC. Under the leadership of Koos de Wet, at Messrs UCDD, the Bosvark II would take shape. Several improvements were identified, and a presentation was made to ARMSCOR early in 1976. A wooden mock-up was completed by April 1976 and presented to officials from SADF, ARMSCOR, the Department of Trade and Industry, and the DRU.

The SADF, with the development of the SAMIL range of vehicles, was planning to phase out the Unimog and subsequent assistance from ARMSCOR for the Bosvark II dried up and the development

Buffel MPVs leaving Angola at the conclusion Operation Displace in August 1988. Originally published in PARATUS, September 1988. (M. Botha)

team had to rely on their own wits and assistance from the DRU to pull the project through. The final prototype was ready by late August 1976 and presented to ARMSCOR and the SADF who required that the vehicle undergo mobility and durability tests.

Messrs UCDD continued its support for the Bosvark II, and the necessary mobility and durability tests were arranged on a farm near Zeerust. Representatives from interested groups attended and put the Bosvark II through its paces from dusk until dawn. Some improvements were identified by the development team, but the Bosvark II was certified as tested. Nine more test vehicles were built and delivered to the SADF for testing in the then Northern Transvaal and Ovamboland and a quotation was requested for more vehicles from UCDD. The CRU (later CDU) of the CSIR, under the direction of Dr Vernon Joynt, made further improvements.

In 1976, a live blast test was arranged, and Koos de Wet was invited to attend to witness the proceedings. Explosives were placed under the front left wheel of the vehicle. In place of a human occupant, a female baboon was drafted for SADF service, drugged, and strapped into the driver's seat. After a massive explosion, the vehicle's left wheel was nowhere to be found. The baboon survived and was given first aid for a cut on its lip. Attendees were

Bosvark Mk1 APC. (CSIR)

Bosvark 2 during mobility and wheel displacement testing. (K. de Wet)

impressed, and the experts agreed that the driver and passengers would survive a mine detonation. Koos de Wet was informed that the vehicle would be called the "*Buffel*" (Buffalo) if it were placed in SADF service. Both Messrs Busaf Border and Messrs Transverse, which contributed to the development, were excluded by the SADF and ARMSCOR from the Buffel production. Further tests were conducted by the SADF and ARMSCOR throughout early to mid-1977 and improvements made.

61 Base Workshop was often called upon to assist in projects and even at times to manufacture and develop prototypes and would become responsible for the disassembly of the SADF Unimog fleet and preparation for its conversion to the Buffel. The first 19 Buffels left Voortrekkerhoogte in Pretoria, South Africa for the major military logistics and supply base at Grootfontein in SWA during the latter half of 1977. The first Buffels were deployed operationally

in 1978, and some 2,985 vehicles would be built over a period of 17 years.

The Buffel Mk1 was fitted with the same Mercedes Benz OM352 6-cylinder water-cooled diesel engine as had been used on the Unimog-based Bosvark and received a bush guard on the front of the vehicle which helped protect it from damage caused by driving through the bush. The Mk1A was improved by being equipped with drum instead of disc brakes and an Atlas diesel 352 6-cylinder water-cooled engine (a licensed copy of the Mercedes Benz engine). The Mk1B and subsequent variants used the same licensed engine and had the drum brakes replaced with disc brakes. If implemented, the Buffel Mk2 would have seen the passenger tub being redesigned with all-round vision through bulletproof windows, an armoured roof, and a rear entry and exit door.

Buffel APC front left side view, at the War and Peace Revival 2019 show. (C. Moore)

Buffel APC rear view, at the War and Peace Revival 2019 show. (C. Moore)

DESIGN FEATURES

The Buffel was designed to maximise its occupants' chances of survival when a mine was detonated anywhere under the hull. This was achieved through several key design elements which included high ground clearance, a V-shaped underbelly, and a purpose-built strengthened upper design which reduced the risk of shattered or buckled hull plates which could become debris.

The African terrain, which in and of itself can inflict severe punishment on a vehicle, necessitated a robust design. The Buffel's design and simplicity made field repairs post-mine detonation possible, although very costly. A chassis-based MPV does not provide the same protection to the vehicle driveline when compared to modern monocoque hull design vehicles. Most parts could be obtained commercially, which made the Buffels' logistical train shorter and specialised maintenance support in the field unnecessary.

Mobility

The Unimog 4×4 chassis was designed for difficult off-road applications in Europe, and this design suited the African battlespace. The suspension consisted of single-coil springs on the front axle and double coil springs on the rear axle. The Buffel had a ground clearance of 420mm (16.5in) and could ford 1m (3ft) of water. The high ground clearance and narrow width made the Buffel somewhat top-heavy, which occasionally caused problems for inexperienced drivers who would roll the vehicle over if they turned too sharply while at speed, or on uneven or wet and slippery terrain. For those not used to the vehicle's sway and motion, the passenger tub was nicknamed the *kots koets* (vomit carriage).

The engine produced 125hp (20.4hp/t) at 2,800rpm and was coupled to an eight-speed (eight forward and four reverse) synchromesh manual transmission, the transfer box of which was integrated with the gearbox. The transmission design allowed for in-motion changing between 2×4 and 4×4-wheel drive and featured an equal 50% front and rear axle power distribution. The four wheels are 12:50x20 in size. As an experiment, each wheel was filled with approximately 60ℓ (15.8gal) of water to help absorb the explosive force from a landmine. Conversely, this added around 300kg (661lb) of weight which negatively affected the vehicle's range and caused other failures to the suspension, wheel bearings and the axle and this idea was soon dropped.

The Buffel would come to serve in virtually all the branches of the SADF until its retirement in 1995. During the full production phase, all of the chassis were produced and assembled in East London and shipped to Rosslyn in Pretoria where the armoured hulls were produced by Steelmobile Engineering and mounted onto the chassis. At one point in time, the production rate was scaled up to six vehicles a day with one shift day. The production price of a complete vehicle was R45,535 in 1983, equivalent to R779,657 today (approximately US$46,000 at the time of writing). Buffel vehicles were also produced for the various Government sectors in SWA such as Water Affairs and the Roads Department and Koevoet/ SWAPOL used some vehicles in the early 1980s before they were issued with the Casspir vehicle. The only foreign country to ever buy Buffels from the South African government directly was Sri Lanka (185). All other users either bought them at SA Army auctions or through the private sector. Only a handful of countries, which include Malawi, Sri Lanka, Uganda, and Zambia, still use the Buffel (or variants thereof).

Endurance and logistics

The Buffel had a 200ℓ (52.8gal) fuel tank which granted it an operational range of 1,000km (600mi) on-road and 500km (300mi) off-road. Its maximum road speed is 96km/h (60mph) and 30km/h (19mph) off-road. A modular design allowed for easier maintenance and reduced logistical requirements and the commercial nature of the components made replacement easy and lowered the costs for parts.

Vehicle layout

The Buffel consisted of three main parts: chassis, armoured driver's cab at the front left of the vehicle, and an armoured passenger tub at the centre rear. The engine is located on the front right-hand side of the vehicle and the transmission in-between the engine and the armoured driver's cab. The engine and transmission placement facilitated easy replacement in the event of damage due to a mine detonation.

The driver's cab is surrounded by three rectangular bulletproof glass windows and has an open-top. The base is wedge-shaped and secured to the chassis via cables. A single door is installed on the left side of the driver's cab, as well as two steel steps for

Buffel APC driver's cab, at the War and Peace Revival 2019 show. (C. Moore)

Buffel APC passenger tub, at the War and Peace Revival 2019 show. (C. Moore)

ease of entrance. Later variants would also receive a high-density polyethylene roof cover over the driver's cab. The gear selection is located on the right-hand side of the driver, and a spare wheel is kept to the right of the driver's cab. The driver's and passenger's seating is blast resistant and designed to protect the spine in case of a mine detonation under the vehicle. The vehicle remained a left-hand drive configuration as the design of the chassis is of German origin.

Access to the passenger tub is gained via two incremental pairs of steel steps on either side. The passenger tub seating is arranged in two rows of five seats, facing outward from the centre. All seats are equipped with harnesses to secure the occupants in the case of a mine detonation or accidental rollover, which would otherwise see them thrown from the vehicle. A further feature is an anti-roll bar over the top of the passenger tub which would stop the passenger tub rolling over completely. The left and right sides of the passenger tub contained a horizontal panel with semi-circular grooves to allow rifle fire from the seated passengers. During contact, the passengers would debus by jumping over the side of the vehicle. The panels are horizontally hinged which allowed them to be opened to ease dismounting. This was, however, rarely done while on the move, as

the panels had a tendency to flip backwards while crossing uneven terrain at speed, which could lead to injury.

Traditionally, the section leader would sit on the front left to facilitate communication with the driver. The section BMG team sat at the rear left with the 2IC, who operated the rear-facing machine gun. The number one rifleman sat in the front right and manned the front-facing machine gun, while the remainder of the section sat on the right.

On the rear of the passenger tub is a sizable storage box manufactured from high-density polyethylene. The front lower part of the storage box was used by the passengers to store spare kit, while the top part was for the driver's use. On occasion, a road-killed warthog would be thrown in the storage box for later consumption. At the rear of the chassis is a water tap which is connected to a 100ℓ (26.4gal) fresh water tank.

Protection

The Buffel could protect its occupants against a single TM-57 anti-tank mine blast under the hull, which was equivalent to 6.34kg (14lb) of TNT, or a double TM-57 anti-tank mine blast under any wheel. Its V-shaped bottom armoured hull design deflected blast energy and fragments away from the driver and passenger tub. The driver's cab windows were all bulletproof. Plastic fuel and water tanks were located within the V-shaped hull of the passenger tub and would help absorb explosive blast energy from a mine detonation. The armoured driver's cab and passenger tub protected against common small arms fire in the theatre, including 7.62mm NATO and 7.62mm AK-47 Ball ammunition as well as explosive fragments.

Main armament
The Buffel's standard armament was either a single or dual pintle-mounted 7.62mm BMG, which was located on the forward right-hand side of the passenger tub and/or rear left-hand side. Twin mountings have also been observed, with the gunners receiving a gun shield as well. In open terrain, this placement was convenient, but when the Buffel entered the thick bush, the primary armament being located forward would get turned around by branches, making their effective use difficult.

The Buffel Family
The Buffel spawned several variants, which included a 2.5t cargo carrier and an ambulance.

Moffel
When the Buffel was deployed in urban operations to quell the ever-increasing civil unrest and factional fighting (1991-1993) in South Africa, a redesign was needed to improve all-round safety. This involved enclosing the driver's cab and passenger tub, which were vulnerable to petrol bombs and other dangerous flying objects. The passenger tub's horizontal drop-down panels were replaced with bulletproof glass windows with two firing ports each for self-defence. A rear access door with a bulletproof window was added to facilitate entry and exit from the tub. Additionally, a bulletproof window was fitted on the forward right side. The passengers can open hatches on the top of the tub. The subsequent redesign of the passenger tub reduced the available space from ten to eight passengers, and the seating faced inwards. The overall improvements allowed better all-round vision but increased the weight by 800kg (1764lb), which was not acceptable for the chassis. A limited number of Moffel vehicles were produced, and the vehicle was limited for road use only. When the Buffel vehicle was withdrawn from service, a total number of 582 Mamba APC vehicles were built utilising the Buffel or Unimog driveline.

Cargo Carrier
Based on the Buffel Mk1B, the Cargo Carrier was produced in the early 1980s. It retained the one-man driver's cab; however, the personnel tub was replaced with an open load bed. It could carry 2.6t of cargo over 900km (559mi). A total of 57 were produced.

Ambulance
Making use of the standard Buffel Mk1B, the Ambulance variant prototype retained the armoured one-man driver's cab at the front. The passenger tub was redeveloped to be enclosed and could accommodate two medical staff, four lying down, and one sitting patient. Access was gained to the passenger tub via a rear door. It was, however, concluded that the swaying motion of the passenger cab would make the treatment of casualties difficult and very uncomfortable, and the vehicle weight increased by 400kg (882lb), which was not acceptable for the chassis. Subsequently, no orders were placed.

MINE INCIDENTS AND NON-CONTACT ACCIDENTS
The Buffel's primary role was to protect its users from landmine blasts. The following statistics show its success in this regard.

Table 1: Certified Buffel mine incidents				
Mine type	Incidents	Killed	Injured	Personnel
Single mines (6kg [13lb] TNT)	206	9	326	-
Double mines (12kg [26lb] TNT)	34	10	111	-
Triple mines (18kg [39lb] TNT)	6	2	16	-
Total number	246	19	453	2,706

Brigadier General (retd) Tony Savides puts the Buffel into perspective:

At the time Buffel was acquired, it was pretty much in line with (then) existing MPV technology and design, i.e. a mine-and ballistic-protected body upon a B-vehicle chassis. A V-shape and height above the blast were key elements of the technology at the time. The monocoque MPVs such as Casspir, Mamba and others came later. The only other section-carrying MPV in SADF series use at that stage was the Hippo; while there were also a number of Bosvark MPVs in service (the latter not exactly meeting the then criteria for MPVs).

The initial role for which MPVs (and thus Buffel) was intended was the protection of an infantry section (or equivalent) on roads in areas where vehicle (or

Moffel APC at the SA Armour Museum. (G.C. Hurley)

tank) mines and ambushes were a threat. All-wheel or off-road drive was a secondary requirement for (a) poor to bad roads and (b) emergency travel off-road – such as in counter-ambush drills and follow-up. Buffel was thus "mine and ambush-protected" and not intended as anything more than a patrol vehicle. The rationale behind the "on roads" use was that, with the exception of minefields and random "nuisance mines", mines were pre-eminently planted on roads used by military personnel and civilians.

However, Buffel's capabilities were such that it was soon being employed in an "aggressive APC role" over and above the more-passive "mine defence role"; and the MPV was used extensively in several cross-border operations in concert with Ratels and later Casspirs. This will; hopefully, one day be the subject of a study and/or a book on the role of the MPVs in the Border War.

The requirement for a more capable MPV was identified almost as Buffel was coming into service and I personally wrote the staff requirement for the MPCV – in essence, a replacement for Buffel in certain roles and to provide a better combat capability. This requirement was binned when Casspir was acquired, and it re-surfaced later as part of other projects; but to date, this requirement has not been satisfied (if it still exists at all). Buffel was retained due to its proven effectiveness.

The acquisition of the Mamba 4x2 and later the conversion of Mamba into a 4x4 using Unimog/Buffel components was a direct result of different APC types being required for internal security operations.

That Buffel may have been used outside its intended role is accepted; but this should have been mitigated by proper training, effective command and control and effective discipline. In many, if not most, photographs of Buffels deployed and moving on roads; there are personnel standing in the back – some even standing on the seats.

The Buffel, having a high centre of gravity, had a dubious reputation for falling over. There were 59 such incidents which resulted in 72 deaths. Some of the possible causes include:

- High centre of gravity
- Body roll at speed, especially on overtaking or when taking evasive action
- Instability caused by personnel in the rear standing instead of being seated
- Instability increased if standing persons moved around
- Speed (higher than safe for the conditions and/or in contravention of SOPs and other orders)
- Reckless driving (too-sharp turns at speed, unnecessary swerving, excessive braking, etc.)
- Showing off by drivers
- Inexperienced drivers and/or commanders

- Inclement weather
- Off-road tyres that grip in a sideways skid on hard roads (rather than slide over the surface)
- Mechanical failures (e.g. one recorded instance of a wheel coming off on the move)
- Poor maintenance
- Under-inflated tyres
- Slippery road surfaces (wet or dusty)
- Different tyre types on a vehicle
- Poor discipline
- Poor command and control
- Heavy items not secured in the hull and which became projectiles on roll-over (although obviously, in certain states or readiness some items had to be free to use)
- It is accepted that contact or follow-up drills may have required speeding-up, swerving and personnel leaving their seats to carry out certain actions. Roll-overs may well have occurred during such actions

Operational history

During the South African Border War, the Buffel was used as a dedicated transport, as well as for logistics and COIN operations as part of combat groups. Sections were transported to designated points, from where they would conduct patrols on foot for between three and seven days before being picked up again or receive replenishment for a further seven days.

A fighting group consisted of between four to six Buffels, which would carry a platoon between them, with one or two Buffels serving as supply/logistics vehicles. Enough food, water, and ammunition were carried for seven days, which covered roughly 600-800km (373-497mi). Replenishment would be done every six days if the patrol was extended.

The Buffel in Action

The Buffel was such a versatile MPV that it was used by every SADF infantry battalion which served in SWA, as well as in every major military operation from Operation Reindeer to the cessation

Buffel Mk1B cargo carrier. (O. Bergh)

of hostilities in 1989. Additionally, it was used in vast numbers for internal security.

32 Battalion, an elite light infantry unit consisting of ex-Angolans under the command of SADF officers and NCOs, received Buffels. Three-two, as they were better known, was most often used for reconnaissance and offensive operations in Angola. Having received Buffels, they became a light motorised unit and during Operation Protea three motorised companies were attached to Combat Group 40. This consisted of one armoured car squadron (Eland 90), a 120mm mortar battery, four anti-tank teams, and two protection platoons (1 Platoon from B Company of 202 Battalion and one other platoon). Combat Group 40 was tasked to find and destroy SWAPO command, training and logistical bases around the town of Xangongo 70km (43mi) north of the SWA border, and secure the town and its bridge.

The attack would be carried out by Combat Team 41 from the northeast and Combat Team 42 from the southeast at around 12:50 on 24 August. The town was defended by layers of trenches and bunkers which needed to be cleared first, followed by the fort and water tower. By 17:30, the bridge was reached and prepared for demolition by the engineers. During the attack, FAPLA and PLAN officers, together with their Soviet military advisors, quickly fled, leaving the soldiers behind to fend for themselves. By 25 August, all Battle Group 40's objectives were reached. On 26 August, they set out to join Task Force Bravo, which was operating to the east against PLAN bases.

CONCLUSION

The Buffel was the first-ever mass-produced open-topped mine-protected V-shaped hull MPV/APC. Although not very comfortable, it fulfilled its role as an MPV by saving the lives of countless SADF soldiers whose vehicles detonated landmines. It became the backbone of many SADF border patrol and COIN operations. The Buffel served for 17 years until it was replaced by the Mamba MPV in 1995. Some 582 Mamba MPVs would be manufactured around rebuilt Buffel drivelines.

A soldier's story with the Buffel 1983/84

During my National Service, I ended up in 1SSB, which is an armoured unit. I always wanted to drive tanks but never got to do that and ended up driving SAMIL trucks instead. Towards the end of the year, we flew from Bloemfontein to Grootfontein and ended up at a camp in Sector 10 Oshakati. After a few weeks of acclimatising to the heat, we were mustered to go into Angola which was the start of Ops Askari.

As I didn't have a vehicle of my own, I accompanied a good friend of mine, Chris Venter and was the sole occupant of the rear compartment of the Buffel, other than rations and supplies. As we crossed the border between Namibia and Angola a guy, whom I knew, jumped onto the back of the Buffel and as we drove over a barbed wire fence, we found ourselves across the border inside Angola. At the time it was a bit of an anti-climax, for some reason we thought it would be more dramatic than it actually was.

During the following weeks, the routine pretty much was the same consisting of driving all day, laagering at dusk and maintaining silence during the evening period. Once the sundown procedure was complete, we would fire up the esbit tablet stoves and proceed to make our evening meal. It was quite amazing just how far a ratpack would go once your stomach got used to the well-balanced diet contained therein. I remember giving Chris a hard time because I didn't think that he was pulling his weight in the evening meal making, he, quite rightly so, gave me a piece of his mind of just how hard it was doing bundu bashing driving throughout the day.

Water was always a priority, and on one occasion a group of us decided to have an ammo box bath, basically sticking your bum in the ammo box and bathing with what little water you had. Needless to say, we were caught out and spent the next two hours doing "afkak" (slang for an attitude adjustment). This consisted of running with a 155mm artillery shell until you couldn't hold it anymore and were sweating more than you were before the punishment. I think there were four of us and as we proceeded to finish the route allocated for us to run and I think I was the last to finish. We were travelling with an artillery detachment manned by SA Cape Corps members, and as I was running past two [of them] the one guy turned to his mate and said "*Nee man! Laat ons die ou help*" (Let's help the guy out.) They both picked up the shell and ran with me to the end. I get emotional still thinking about the kindness and camaraderie of that small gesture. The routine was that at 21h00 the artillery would open up and fire a salvo at the enemy and on one occasion I managed to fall asleep under a truck, and as the guns opened up for the night, I jerked awake and bashed my head against the truck's diff.

Trooper

(retd) S. Tegner

Buffel Ambulance prototype. (Author's collection)

A soldier's story with the Buffel 1986

Sometime during March 1986, we were again working with a combined intelligence group under the command of a Captain Maree? This time we were east of Oshikango and gathering information on SWAPO movement, as well as the area east and south-east of Ongiva in Angola. It is the rainy season, and the sand was very thick and wet. Here one of the Buffalo's weaknesses came to the fore, and it was the gear levers that were not strong enough and perhaps too thin. You have to pull away in first gear all the way down (4x4) and switch to second gear as quickly as possible to build momentum. The effects were with the quick jerk/shift of the gear lever; then the lever breaks down where it is secured with two u-bolts to the section above the gearbox. If you were lucky enough, your Buffalo had three gear lever/handle switches, namely the first to fourth gear lever, low and cough gear lever and forward and reverse gear. Unfortunately, most Buffels had only two levers, namely the first to fourth gear and the forward and reverse gear. If the gear lever broke from the first to fourth link, you then took it off and replaced it with one of the others to switch at least from first to fourth, after you first had [hit] the lever with a hammer bite to bend it more or less the same as the original lever.

Buffel APC after a double cheese mine (stacked mines) detonation in 1981. (G. Korff)

Flat wheels were a problem due to all the driving done off-road. I had four flat wheels in three days but was able to repair a tire fairly quickly. Unfortunately, we did not have a logistics vehicle with us with spare tires, and the immediate repair of a flat tire was vital. The biggest problem was getting the spare tire from its position next to the engine and then put the other tire back there. If you positioned yourself correctly, you could do it alone, but often a few extra hands made it much easier to get that heavy tire back there. There was supposed to be some kind of mechanical hand winch to help you ease the task that moved right into the top of the Buffalo bin, but most of the Buffel[s] we drove didn't have it anymore, or the pulleys had broken.

During the week that followed, the war also took on a new reality for me. SWAPO had always been the invisible enemy, except for the corpses that were brought by Koevoet and other teams to the base for burial. We received information early one morning that a group of five had moved close by our base. We found their tracks and then caught them half-unexpectedly with their temporary overnight base. They fled, but left behind a lot of their equipment, including backpacks with clothes and a lot of ammunition such as RPG rockets and some 81mm mortars. They split into two groups, and it was decided to follow the group of three rather than the other two. It would be a long day to track them, but our Bushmen and Owambo trackers were excellent at their job.

The trackers went ahead with the rest of our soldiers spread outwards and backwards. Then our drivers with the Buffalo followed much further behind with only a few men at the back who sometimes rotated with some of the others on the ground. We usually had to watch the soldiers on the ground in front of us at a distance and then follow them. It is not always an easy task if the bush becomes rougher and eyesight is sometimes very limited. I still don't know how far the SWAPOs were in front of us and whether the trackers may have lost track of them, but late in the afternoon, Captain Maree informed us that we were still going to follow the tracks for a while, then stopped and executed a firing plan in a certain direction, turning in another direction, driving for an hour or so and then set up a temporary base for the night.

Less than half an hour later, there was an explosion with a lot of gunfire coming from the front. I thought it was the fire plan being executed, but the soldiers in the back of the Buffel suddenly shouted that I should rush forward. I still wanted to argue, but it became clear that there was trouble ahead. Rushing forward a 100m (109yd) with the Buffel the troops jump off the back and starts running forward in a combat formation and lays down suppressing fire.

It turned out that one of the trackers walked into a trap and stepped on a Pom-Z anti-personnel landmine. The soldiers immediately around him went down and began firing in various directions to keep SWAPO's heads down if they planned to shoot or flee.

One does not realize how much damage a fairly small anti-personnel mine can do, but it is a vicious weapon designed to cripple people. The tracker's leg was in a terrible state, and to this day, I don't know if he may have lost a leg or foot. Another eight soldiers also sustained serious and less serious shrapnel wounds as a result of that mine blast. My respect for medics took on a new dimension. The medic who was with us jumped into action trying to help the wounded even though he suffered a minor shrapnel wound himself. Here, too, I gained more respect for Captain Maree, who was in charge of our group. I had no idea where we were, but he knew and did his job as a leader well. He determined our position and radio[ed] Ondangwa for a helicopter evacuation for the wounded.

A quick helicopter landing zone was prepared and an all-round defence. The Puma helicopter flew towards us straight and very low, loaded up the wounded and disappeared just as fast and low back again south across the "*Kaplyn*" (border between SWA and Angola). It was quite impressive how accurately they could fly in and fly out at a time before the modern navigation aids such as GPS.

We continued our drive in Angola until late at night and then made a temporary base for the rest of the night. We went on the intelligence operation for another two days before turning south again and returned to Ondangwa without any further incidents, except for another flat tire or two and no working brakes on my Buffel.

The next month or so until mid-April, we continued with our usual tasks such as taking the medical ordinance [to] Oshikati, further intelligence patrols in the areas around Ondangwa without any incidents, until our time in SWA was complete, and we returned to South Africa.

Lance Corporal (retd) N. Ferreira

3
Ratel Infantry Combat Vehicle

THE AFRICAN BUSH FIGHTER

The Ratel ICV takes its Afrikaans name from the South African honey badger. This animal, despite its small size, is a fierce creature which is able to absorb a large amount of physical damage as well as dish it out with its long claws. The Ratel vehicle is therefore well named as its armament and mobility make it a formidable opponent.

DEVELOPMENT

During the mid-1960s there was a growing realisation in the SADF that foreign imported armoured troop vehicles, such as the Saracen, were not up to the task against modern threats and the requirements based on the challenges found in the Southern African battlespace. What was needed was a highly manoeuvrable, ultra-reliable and

Ratel 12.7 – Operation Hooper. (C van Schoor)

easy to maintain ICV, armed to the teeth, which could fulfil the doctrine requirements being developed by the SADF for mobile warfare. Project *Pampoen* (Pumpkin) as it would later become known, would eventually fulfil this stated requirement which was translated into a user requirement in 1970. In 1972, South African company Springfield Büssing presented a 6x6 APC built by MAN for trials. It would later be named Buffel (not to be confused with the Buffel APC described in Chapter 2). Of the five contenders, the Springfield Büssing Buffel was found to be the most suitable and would after another year and two more evaluation trials serve as the developmental platform for designing the Ratel.

Springfield Büssing Buffel on display at 1 SAI. (D. Venter)

The first prototype, Ratel SS, was made of mild steel which allowed quicker modification work. Although the exterior resemblance between the Buffel and Ratel SS are noticeable, the Ratel SS was a completely different beast. Testing on the Ratel SS was done over a five-month period in 1974 and the first four production Ratels were put through their paces at the Elandsfontein vehicle testing grounds near Pretoria in 1975. The first batch of 13 Ratel Mk1s was delivered from the production line at Sandock-Austral in Boksburg in 1975 followed by series production. After operational field experience, several improvements were made which enhanced the Ratel's bush breaking capability. Some of the changes included adding large covers to protect external headlights which were initially covered by mesh wire, and a screen cover to keep leaves from being sucked into the engine. These modifications were only later designated as the Mk3 standard.

The Ratel 20 can be seen as the base model from which the Ratel family was produced. The

Ratel SS on display at 1 SAI. (D. Venter)

Ratel 20 Mk3 on public display. (G.C. Hurley)

Ratel 90 Mk3 on public display. (G.C. Hurley)

Ratel 12.7 Mk3 Command on public display. (G.C. Hurley)

preferred but would eventually not see the light of day. After some trial and error, the first Ratel 81 was delivered in mid-1985. The first operational deployment occurred during Operation Benzine. The need for a mobile anti-tank missile capability was identified in the early 1960s which led to South Africa acquiring the Milan AT missiles during the early to mid-1970s. Being wire-guided, their use in the African bush was limited as their guiding wire would get caught in the bush, and targets could easily move out of sight before the missile reached them. A domestically built laser-guided missile would be much more suitable, and development was undertaken by Kentron in the late 1970s. By 1986 the development was complete, and the ZT3 missile systems were ready for industrialisation. A Ratel 20 hull would be used, and the specially designed turret and ZT3 missile system mounted thereon.

The final upgrade of the Ratel family of vehicles to the Mk3 standard was implemented in 1985 and included more than 135 modifications, such as an improved cooling system, additional fuel filters, digital acceleration meter and more robust bush protection, e.g. by moving the front exterior lights lower and strengthening the steps to enter and exit the vehicle.

The Ratel family of vehicles allowed the SADF the mobility needed from 1976 onwards as the South African Border War escalated and cross-border operations became more frequent and more complex. The primary liberation movement for SWA, SWAPO, conducted increasingly-daring cross-border sabotage, intimidation and assassination raids from their bases in Angola into SWA. Ratels, with their high speed and endurance, were employed to intercept SWAPO raiders when they crossed the border. High-mobility operations saw Ratel formations often consisting of battalion-sized columns with mixtures of other South African-produced military vehicles (Buffel, Eland, SAMIL etc.) leaving their bases located near the northern border of SWA to conduct deep incursions into Angola against SWAPO training and logistic camps.

production of the Ratel 12.7 Command commenced in 1979/1980 after completing its evaluation and testing successfully. The need for an anti-tank vehicle was already expressed in September 1974 and by early 1979 an Eland 90 turret was fitted to a strengthened Ratel 20 hull, thus giving birth to the Ratel 90. Live fire tests were successful, and more were ordered. The Ratel 90 would first see combat during Operation Sceptic as part of Battle Group 61. The Ratel 60 was conceived in 1980/1981 as a stop-gap due to a shortage of Ratel 20s, due in turn to a shortage of GIAT F2 20mm guns. The decision was made to fit an Eland 60 turret on a Ratel 20 hull, which only took an hour. Conceived in 1977, work on the Ratel 81 only began at the start of 1983, as another project with similar capability was

These cross-border operations by South Africa often targeted SWAPO bases. The MPLA and the Angolan conventional army, FAPLA, were only attacked if they interfered. The war escalated as Cuba, backed by Soviet advisors, sent troops and equipment to aid the MPLA and FAPLA. The SADF doctrine of mobile warfare made maximum use of the Ratel's characteristics and allowed them to influence the flow of the war and they often outmanoeuvred numerically superior adversaries.

Ratel 60 Mk3 on public display. (G.C. Hurley)

Since its introduction in 1974 and subsequent evolution of variants, the Ratel family of vehicles formed the backbone of all mechanised operations by the then SADF during the South African Border War. They were fielded with SADF units such as 61 Mech, 32 Battalion and 4 and 8 SAI Battalions. Other units that made use of the Ratel included Citizen Force Mechanised Infantry units as well as other branches of the SADF such as artillery, engineers and signals. It played an integral role during the 1998 SADC intervention in Lesotho, which was led by the SANDF, and various UN peacekeeping forces have made use of the Ratel in conflict zones. Some 1,381 Ratels were built. Since 1994, Ratels have also been exported to Cameroon, Djibouti, Ghana, Jordan, Libya, Morocco, Rwanda, Sahrawi Arab Democratic Republic, Senegal, Yemen and Zambia. Exported Ratels have also been used during the Libyan Civil War, Yemeni Revolution and Yemeni Crisis (2011 – present).

Ratel ZT3 PPM on public display. (G.C. Hurley)

For a complete history of the Ratel, Botha's *Ratel: The making of a legend* (see bibliography) is strongly recommended.

DESIGN FEATURES

The Ratel was the best vehicle ever made for the ultra-mobile African bush warfare. The terrain it operated in is some of the most hostile in the world, which alone inflicts harsh punishment. Characterised by its massive wheels, swiftness, bush breaking ability and versatility as a weapons platform, it was a fearsome adversary in skilled hands during the South African Border War.

Major General (retd) Roland de Vries

Mobility

The Ratel is of a 6x6 wheeled configuration, characterised by its versatility and cross-country capability optimised for the African battlespace. It makes use of 14:00x20 run-flat tyres (designed to resist the effects of deflation when punctured). The Ratel uses the Büssing D 3256 BTXF six-cylinder direct-injection turbocharged diesel engine which produces 282hp (210kW) at 2,400rpm. This provides a 14.9hp/t power to combat weight ratio for the Ratel 20. The engine is located at the rear left of the vehicle and proved more than sufficient to navigate off-road and to push through dense bush and small trees. The power pack can be field stripped and replaced in roughly 30 minutes by two men using a crane. The engine is coupled to an automatic powershift gearbox containing a hydrodynamic torque converter which eases driving. The gearbox is automatic but can also be operated manually and has a mechanical emergency gearshift. Gear selection ranges from automatic, five forward, a neutral and two reverse gears. The power is transmitted to the three axles in two stages with a final decrease using planetary gearing, which is located in the wheel hubs. Each of the three axles has its own lockable differential, and there are longitudinal differential locks. The suspension utilises progressive acting coil springs as well as large hydraulic shock absorbers. The Ratel has 350mm (13.8in) of ground clearance and can ford 1.2m (3.9ft) unprepared. Early trials showed that the Ratel was as amphibious as a brick. Surprisingly, on that occasion, the engine kept running underwater until the Ratel was rescued from its water baptism. The Ratel also has the distinction of sometimes becoming semi-airborne, but that will be left for another publication. The maximum recommended safe road

ZT3A1 missile, with a single shaped charge warhead, on public display. (G.C. Hurley)

speed is 80km/h (50mph), but Ratel can achieve 120km/h (75mph) unofficially. Cross-country and terrain dependant, the Ratel can achieve 40km/h (25mph). The Ratel can cross a 1.15m (3.8ft) ditch at a crawl and can climb a 60% gradient. It is equipped with three beam axles, coil springs, and shock-absorbers.

Endurance and logistics

The fuel capacity of the Ratel is 480ℓ (37.5gal) which allows it to travel 1,000km (621mi) by road and 600km (372mi) off-road and enables flexible force movement in order to achieve surprise. Some Ratels were equipped with three 7.62mm BMGs; one mounted co-axially left of the primary weapon, one on the turret structure, above the commander's station for close protection from ground threats, and one to the right rear of the hull for close in anti-air support. Most only had the co-axial and the AA mount. The latter was found to be ineffective in its role and proved better in the close-in ground defence role. The average number of 7.62mm BMG rounds carried is at least 6,000.

A B-56 long-range and a B-26 short-range radio are located at the rear of the turret for tactical communication and reliable command and control, enhancing the ICV's force multiplier effect on the battlefield. The effective communication between Ratel 90s allowed the well trained SADF crews to attack and defeat T-54/55 MBTs during various South African Border War operations.

The Ratel would undertake missions over rugged and variable terrain with little logistical support. It needed to be, and was, well-armed and self-sustaining, carrying its own supplies, some spare parts and a section of infantry. Spare wheels were lashed to the roof of the hull, while the food was stored in every available space (as well as a few cases of beer). Spare whip aerials for the radios were always carried somewhere on the hull as they had a tendency to break when driving through the brush. The Ratel featured two built-in drinking water tanks which stored a total of 100ℓ (26gal). Additional jerry cans were carried based on operational requirements and stored where there was a room available. The overall emphasis was on self-sufficiency, from fire support to first aid. A platoon of Ratels could remain self-sufficient for three days.

Vehicle layout

The Ratel was the first wheeled ICV to ever be mass-produced and see subsequent service. It features a proper commander's cupola which offers a 360-degree field of vision. The commander is located on the left side of the turret while the gunner sits on the right. Entry and exit for the former and latter are through the gunner's and vehicle commander's hatches respectively. In an emergency, the gunner and vehicle commander can escape through the rear of the vehicle. The driver's compartment is located at the front and centre of the vehicle, from where he has an excellent 270-degree vision through three large bulletproof windows. During the battle, the driver can activate three armoured shields which pop up to cover the windows for extra protection. When the armoured shields are activated, the driver uses three day-periscopes with a view to the front, left and right. The driver can enter and exit the vehicle from either a roof hatch located above his seat or through the interior of the vehicle. The driver makes use of a hydraulically- supported steering wheel which controls the front two wheels and foot pedals for acceleration and braking. All Ratels can be fitted with a small crane jib or tow bar at the rear which can be used to tow a damaged vehicle.

Ratel ZT3-A2s on public display. (R. Fouche)

The hull has entry doors on the left and right of the mid hull which is operated by a hydraulic system to ensure the doors close at any angle; while the door at the rear of the hull is manumatic. The Ratel has several roof hatches (the number being variant dependant) which can be used for employment of personal weapons and grenades, for loading, and for emergency exiting should the need arise.

A Ratel 20 carries a standard complement of three crew (vehicle commander, gunner and driver) and up to eight soldiers. The Ratel's interior can be considered crowded yet, although not standard procedure, space can be found for an additional three passengers when required. The mounted soldiers sit back to back, allowing them to fire through several firing ports located on either side of the vehicle. All seats are fitted with safety belts to ensure that the passengers are not thrown about while the vehicle is moving over rough terrain. The section leader in a Ratel 20 is also the vehicle commander. The Ratel carries four 81mm smoke grenade launchers, two on either side of the turret.

The Ingwe ZT3A2 missile, with tandem shaped charge warhead, on public display. (D. Venter)

Ratel 81 Mk3 on public display. (G.C. Hurley)

Main armament

The Ratel 12.7 Command is equipped with a turret which houses a 12.7mm BMG, a standard coaxial 7.62mm BMG and an additional 7.62 BMG on top of the turret. Some 300x12.7mm rounds are carried as standard.

The Ratel 20 is fitted with a dual-feed GI-2 20mm quick-firing gun which is a licensed copy of the French GIAT F2 gun and produced in South Africa by LEW, which later became Denel Land Systems. The gun's primary purposes are to lay down sustained suppressive fire, engage enemy troops and to destroy soft-skinned and lightly armoured enemy vehicles. The gun can elevate between -8 degrees and +38 degrees and can fire are a rate of 750 rounds per minute (12.5 rounds a second). The auto-feed mechanism allows with a flip of a switch the immediate change between the two different ammunition belts (of 150 rounds each) feeding into the gun. The primary ammunition types used were 20x139mm HE-I and APCT. The HE-I travels at 1,050m/s (3,448ft/s) and is effective up to 2km (1.2mi). The APCT rounds travel at 1,300m/s (4,265ft/s) and are considered effective up to 1km (0.6mi) but can penetrate 15mm (0.6in) of RHA at zero degrees at 2km (1.2mi). A total of 1,200 20mm rounds are carried in total.

The Ratel 60 makes use of the Eland 60 turret and retained the short 60mm M2 breech-loading gun mortar and the standard coaxial 7.62mm BMG. It can fire a 1.72kg (3.8lb) bomb at 200m/s (656ft/s) up to 300m (328yd) in the direct role or 2km (1.2mi) in the indirect role. The main weapon can elevate from -11 to +75 degrees. The 60mm mortar can fire HE, canister, smoke and illuminating rounds and the vehicle carries 45 mortar bombs.

The Ratel 90 is equipped with the same turret and 90mm GT-2 gun as the Eland 90. It makes use of HEAT-T, HE and canister rounds. The HEAT-T round travels at 760m/s, (2,493ft/s), has an effective usage range of 1.2km (0.8mi), and can penetrate up to 320mm (12.6in) of RHA at zero degrees and 150mm (5.9in) at a 60-degree angle. The HE round travels at 650m/s (2133ft/s), is accurate up to 2.2km (1.36mi) and weighs 5.27kg (11.2lb). The 90mm gun can elevate between -8 degrees to +15 degrees and can rotate a full 360 degree in 25 seconds. It carries 50 main weapon rounds, which was a vast improvement over the Eland 90.

The Ratel 81 is equipped with an 81mm mortar firing through a roof hatch located in the centre of the vehicle. The 81mm mortar is mounted on a turntable with can traverse a full 360 degrees. If the

Ratel EAOS Mk2 at the SA Armour Museum. (G.C. Hurley)

Ratel Logistics on display at 1 SAI. (D. Venter)

loaded into the tubes through the Ratel's roof hatch.

Fire control system

The gunners of the Ratel 12.7, Ratel 20, Ratel 60, and Ratel 90 make use of an Eloptro x6 magnification gunner's day sight. Laying the main armament is accomplished via hand-crank while sighting by the gunner is done via a telescopic sight linked to the main gun. The main armament is not stabilised due to the lack of a turret drive. During combat in the South African Border War, this required exceptional skill from the Ratel 90s working in concert to engage enemy targets as quickly as possible while minimizing their exposure to return fire before withdrawing.

The ZT3-A1 and A2 are the only Ratel variants with an electric turret drive, though rotation speed and elevation arcs are not known. The gunner makes use of a dual control stick target tracking system to guide the missile to its target. Its gunner's optical and digital magnification is not known although it could be reasonably argued that the ZT3-A1 uses as a minimum an Eloptro x6.

In the ZT3-A1 targeting is done via traditional gunner's sight while in the ZT3-A2, the gunner makes use of a digital monitor. Additionally, while the ZT3-A1 is equipped with night vision sights, the ZT3-A2 is also equipped with thermal sights.

need arises, the 81mm mortar can be removed for use outside the vehicle. Some 148 mortar bombs are carried although this can be increased by carrying additional containers.

The Ratel ZT3-A1 can fire the ZT3A1 Swift missile which is marketed overseas as the ZT3. The Swift has a minimum range of 250m (273yd), a maximum standoff range of 4km (2.5mi), and its maximum speed is 240m/s (787ft/s). It featured a shaped charge which can penetrate 600mm (23.5in) of RHA at zero degrees. The Ratel ZT3-A2 can fire the newer ZT3A2 "Ingwe" (Leopard) missile which is marketed internationally as the ZT35. Its minimum range is the same as the Swift missile but has a standoff range of beyond 5km (3.1mi) and a maximum speed of 220m/s (722ft/s). The Ingwe features a tandem warhead to counter ERA and can penetrate 1,000mm (3.3ft) of RHA at zero degrees. The missile makes use of laser beam riding to reach its target, which makes it highly resistant to jamming. The Ratel ZT3 missile system is mounted on a modified Ratel 60 turret and carries three missiles ready to use. A total of 12 missiles are carried inside the hull and are manually

Protection

The Ratel was designed for speed and mobility at the cost of armour. The lower nose plate is 20mm (0.79in), angled at 30 degrees while the upper nose is 10mm (0.39in) angled at 75 degrees. The upper hull sides are 8mm (0.31in) at 25 degrees and the lower hull is 10mm (0.39in). The rear hull is 10mm (0.39in), the top of the hull is 6mm (0.24in) and hull floor is 8mm (0.31in). The frontal arc offers protection against 12.7mm AP rounds, however, the upper hull cheeks can be penetrated. The rest of the hull is sufficiently protected against shrapnel and 7.62mm AP rounds. Ratels are extremely susceptible to fire from Russian-supplied 23mm anti-aircraft weapons which were often employed in a ground defence role by the MPLA and Cuban forces. Contrary to popular belief, the Ratel, although designed with the threat of mines in mind, does not feature a V-shaped underbelly and its mine resistance is derived from the hull's height above the ground due to its large oversized wheels. The wheels are also designed to blow off and thereby disperse explosive energy, and the wheel arches form a V-shape which helps deflect mine blasts. During the South African Border War, only one mine fatality was recorded when a Ratel drove over a double anti-tank mine which detonated under the belly of the vehicle during Operation Meebos.

THE RATEL FAMILY

The Ratel vehicle platform served as the basis for an entire family of ICVs which form the backbone of the South African mechanised armed forces and includes the Ratel 12.7, Ratel 20, Ratel 60, Ratel 90, Ratel 81, Ratel 120 (prototype), Ratel ZT-3, Ratel Ambulance (field modification), Ratel Log (prototype), Ratel EAOS, Ratel EW (field modification) and the Ratel Recovery (field modification).

Ratel 12.7

The smaller 12.7mm main weapon allows for a more spacious turret interior compared to the Ratel 20. The Ratel Command carries the standard three-man crew (vehicle commander, driver and main gunner) with space for six command post personnel. The troop compartment is fitted with map tables and communication equipment to fulfil its designed role specifications and to keep the additional communications equipment from overheating an air-conditioning system was fitted. Ratel 20 Command and Ratel 60 Command variants were also produced.

Ratel 20

The Ratel 20 carries three crew members and can accommodate anywhere from eight to eleven mounted infantry (mission dependent) in line with the doctrine of offensive operations, which requires rapid closing with and destruction of the enemy. Reumech would later supply the Irish Army with Ratel 20 turrets for their AMLs.

Ratel 60

One Ratel 60 is typically assigned to an armoured car troop for the purpose of fire support and anti-ambush and the vehicle most often operated from the rear to supply indirect fire.

Ratel 90

The Ratel 90 was based on the Ratel 20 and mounts a turret with a low velocity 90mm gun, identical to the Eland 90 which it replaced in the ant-tank and fire support role.

Further changes involved the reworking of the roof lining and a reduction of the troop compartment roof hatches from four to two to accommodate the turret overhang. The Ratel 90 also carries only one additional crew member (in the mechanised infantry units) and none extra in the armoured car units. This makes room for more ammunition for its main gun with the installation of extra ammunition racks.

The Ratel 90 was developed as both an anti-tank vehicle and a fire support vehicle and proved more than a match for the T-34/85s encountered early on during the South African Border War. As from 1981, the stakes were raised when FAPLA received T-54/55 and T-62 tanks from the Soviet Union and Cuba. Mechanised Infantry Groups fielding Ratel 90s achieved success by skilfully outmanoeuvring the newer Soviet tanks which sometimes required multiple hits with 90mm HEAT rounds from their 90mm guns, often at point-blank range at vulnerable points (engine vents, turret rings) in order to disable them.

Ratel 81

The first four prototypes of the Ratel 81 were delivered to 1 SAI on 12 November 1985. The Ratel 81 has a commander's cupola where the turret would usually be located. This version only has two firing ports on either side of the vehicle. Besides the standard three-man crew, the Ratel 81 carries the three-man mortar team. The vehicle mostly operates from within the combat group to supply indirect fire through shoot and scoot tactics.

Ratel 120

The Ratel 120 was a Ratel 81 fitted with a 120mm mortar with only a few modifications necessary. Successful tests were conducted in 1993 at Alkantpan, which showed that the 120mm mortar firing at maximum charge had no negative effect on the Ratel's suspension system. No Ratel 120 vehicles were produced beyond the prototype.

Ratel ZT3

The ZT3 is a dedicated anti-armour, support, and reconnaissance vehicle and is equipped with a state of the art 127mm (5in) anti-tank missile system developed under Project Raleigh. Due to international sanctions, the SADF had no anti-tank missile which could effectively deal with modern main battle tanks. The South Africans produced the Swift missile and launch system, which was developed to bridge the said gap and the Ratel ZT3 was the end result of the marriage of the Ratel and Swift missile system. This was the first truly modern anti-tank system in the South African military inventory which could engage and destroy modern MBTs. The Ratel ZT3 made its combat debut, while still at a pre-production stage, in September 1987 as part of Operation Moduler, when four pre-production ZT3 vehicles were assigned to 32 Battalion. One of the ZT3 vehicles destroyed three T-54/55 MBTs at 2,000m in the space of 10 minutes. During 2005 the SANDF upgraded 13 ZT3-A1 to ZT3-A2 standard as part of Project Adrift. Some 40 ZT3 vehicles are still in service. The ZT3-A2s missile launcher can fire the newer Ingwe missile and is retro-compatible with the Swift missile system, while the ZT3-A1 launcher can only fire the Swift. The Ratel ZT3-A1 is equipped with night vision sights for the gunner while the ZT3-A2 has been equipped with thermal imaging to maximise its lethality during night-time operations.

Ratel Ambulance

The Ratel Ambulance was not initially part of the official Ratel project but was rather a field modification. It was fielded for the first time during operations Reindeer and Sceptic. It consisted of a converted Ratel 20 hull for medical trauma usage and carried the associated equipment for such a task.

Ratel Log (Logistic)

Unlike the other Ratel variants, the Log was designed as an 8x8 wheeled vehicle which could keep pace with is mechanised family. The Ratel Log would have carried sufficient supplies to support a Ratel platoon for a week during high-intensity operations or two weeks for low-intensity operations. Some 100 Ratel Log vehicles were ordered, but none were produced due to budget constraints.

Ratel EAOS

The main feature of the Ratel EAOS is that it has a hydraulically operated mast but no turret. The mast can be raised to 30m (98ft) off the ground and enables the vehicle to avoid exposing itself. The mast features a sensor package including a video camera system for day and night use, a long-range zoom lens, a FLIR viewer, a

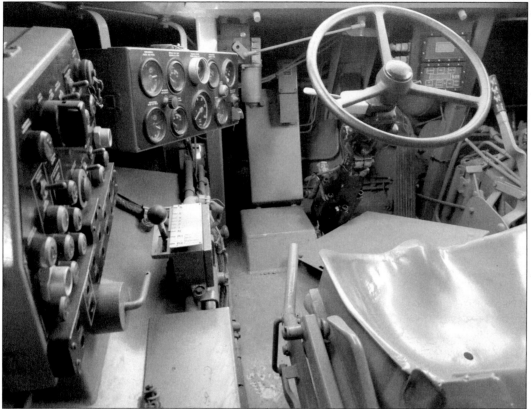

Ratel driver's compartment. (D. Venter)

Ratel 90 ammunition rack in the rear of the turret. (D. Venter)

Ratel Recovery

The Ratel Recovery was a field modification introduced during Operation Reindeer which used a modified Ratel 20 hull fitted with a recovery frame.

CONCLUSION

The Ratel was the first true wheeled ICV to enter military service anywhere in the world and for its time was one of the best ICVs anywhere. It is regarded by most military analysts as the grandfather of all subsequent ICV designs. The Ratel became the backbone of the SADF mechanised battalions and served with distinction during 12 of the 26 years of the South African Border War. In an interview with LITNET in 2013, Major General (retd) Roland de Vries summarised the Ratel (translated from Afrikaans):

> The Ratel was remarkable. If we didn't have the Ratel in Angola during the 80s, we would not now have peace in our land. The Ratel was much more than a weapon. The combination of firepower, mobility, armour protection and flexibility in its application allowed the vehicle itself to be an integrated combat system.

> The Ratel has left a legacy of 44-years of service with which few other military vehicles can compete. The Ratel is now in its final operational service stretch. The SANDF, through Project Hoefyster, has chosen to replace two mechanised battalions of Ratels with the Patria family of ICV vehicles being produced in South Africa and are aptly named Badger.

laser designator, and a laser rangefinder with a video channel. This system allows for accurate observation at 20km (12.4mi) during the day and up to 3.5km (2.2mi) at night. A vehicle-mounted computer system manages the incoming data and computes required firing solutions. The EAOS forms the backbone of the SANDF Artillery Arm's ability for accurate target observation and identification.

Ratel EW

During the latter stages of the South African Border War, a need arose for a dedicated EW capability during forward operations. The SACS operated several converted Ratels with EW equipment.

A soldier's story with the Ratel 90 – Surprise

During Operation Protea, I was assigned to 61 Mech, Combat Group 20. After the main attack on Xangongo airport, we were busy mopping up the trenches and bunkers clearing what we could as darkness caught us. As a result, we had to wait for the morning before we could carry on. There was a sand road nearby where we took up an all-round defence and formed a laager (a protective box formation). After bombing up our Ratels with ammo, cleaning our weapons and eating our rat packs, we went to sleep. Around 0300 we heard a massive sound of vehicles approaching us from the south travelling north. The Ratel 90s were facing east near to the sand road. There were two enemy convoys of trucks carrying troops, ammunition and with field guns. All of us were ready for action in a matter of seconds. The enemy did not see us and drove right passed us till the lead truck came in line at the end of our larger. We received the order to open fire on the double. The trucks exploded with the biggest firework display I have ever seen. A huge fireball mushroom lit up the sky and shrapnel was flying all over the place, pinging off the Ratel's armoured hull. Only when daylight broke did we see the massive destruction that took place.

Corporal (retd) M. Hume
Olifant Mk1A Driver

Ratel ZT3-A2 – Missile stowing racks. (D. Venter)

A soldier's story with the Ratel 90 – First tank kill

This is a story of Toffie Grové and his Ratel 90 crew, 61 Mech, Combat Group 20 during Operation Protea.

On 24 August 1981, late morning the ground attack began on Xangongo from the east moving west with the support of fighter aircraft and artillery fire. Intelligence would indicate the presence

Battle Group 20 advances towards Xangongo during Operation Protea. (M Hume)

of enemy tanks which were dug into a hull-down position south of the town facing south. As Toffie's Ratel 90 fought through the objective, the infantry were clearing the trenches. An infantryman frantically used hand signals to point out a T-34/85 medium tank advancing on Toffie's Ratel 90. Having now seen the approaching tank the Ratel 90 let loose with a HE round which was already loaded for use against soft targets. The HE round had no effect upon hitting. Before the T-34/85 could get its own gun on target, the Ratel 90 loaded a HEAT round and fired. The T-34/85 was hit on the left side of the turret, killing the tank commander. Toffie and his crew were the first to knock out an enemy tank with a Ratel 90 during the South African Border War.

Corporal (retd) M. Hume

A soldier's story with the Ratel 81 – Mortar madness with 62A

It somehow becomes a requirement for some people to have a ritual before going to battle. Like the aircraft pilots in WWII

who would have a little toy strapped to their leg or the bullet that was lodged in the windscreen that never got to them, (in some of the Ratels this was an RPG that got stuck there). In all cases, it is the person who decided that they need a good luck charm or talisman. For 62A1, we had a group ritual, and it wasn't tying lucky things to our arse or legs, we merely asked a question to whoever decided what should happen in the universe. It was a simple question, namely "is it our time?", or in Afrikaans, "*Is dit ons tyd?*" Nothing too hard, a simple question that could be answered in a simple way.

Don't ask me where, or how, or who started it I know our "*Loot*" [Lieutenant] laid the seed of thought, but we got to a stage when we were out of camp and bored, where we would all converge by Crab's seat (on the right of the cabriolet car [our Ratel 81]) and, taking a daily rota one of us would sit in Crab's seat, pick a HE bomb out of the rack and pass it to the group standing in a semi-circle. The bomb was passed from picker to the next person, with the person asking "is it our time?" Five times this happened

A T-34/85, one of many FAPLA tanks captured during the South African Border War. School of Armour, Tempe. (H. Louw)

Ratel 81 Mk3 – 62A of 63 Mech Battalion, Platoon 2, Lohatla, July 1989. (S. Benyon and G. Van Wesemael)

Platoon 2 – "Then it would have been our time". (S. Benyon)

until the person at the end had the bomb. Whoever was in Crab's seat would get down out of the seat and join the group, or poke his head out of the door to have a look, his decision. Then, the appointed last man would knock the bomb on its priming fuse (the nose cone) against the Ratel. After this, the bomb would be returned back to its brethren inside the racks with each person taking over saying "no". A simple ritual, once this was done, 62A1

went back to the daily tasks having no fear from the gods of fortune that day.

Now, readers, you're probably asking why we did this, plus other reasons for this strange ritual, well, when we got the new "Corp" (Corporal) and "Loot" from our intake and the new "Corp" had just taken his place in our cabriolet car. So, first thing in the morning, we were in an exercise, and that meant the artillery (aka Big Guns) was behind us, one missed charge from them lot as the 155mm gun went off and our lives would be little more than dust in the wind. Therefore the ritual was on; we were in danger of being killed, so we congregated around the Number Three's door, Crab's lair. By chance it was Crab's turn, he was in the seat while the rest of us were in a semi-circle around. We even had the new Corp on top of the Ratel standing on my bed (OK, the turntable) looking at his troops and probably thinking what are they doing?

Crab took out the 81mm HE bomb from the rack and passed it to the plotter, whilst asking "is it our time?" The plotter then gave it to Jenks, but also asking "is it our time?" Jenks passed it to me, "is it our time?" Taking the bomb I clearly remember looking up at our new Corp as I passed the bomb to our driver, he was resting his torso on the Ratel, arms folded looking at our ritual with a bemused look on his face. "Is it our time?" I asked. I passed the bomb to our driver but kept an eye on what the Corp would do. Our driver took the bomb, asking "is it our time?" and hit the nose of it pretty hard against the side of the Ratel.

The Corp shat his pants. If anybody could be given a medal for getting your body out of the way, then our Corp would have had the Victorian Cross with Oakleaves, Honoris Crux and a Knights Cross for good luck. One second he was there, the next he was swearing at us. I remember "fuckin mad" and "you fucker" in between several preverbal Afrikaans profanities *"fokkin'"*, *"bliksem"* and *"moertoe"*. In short, the Corp shat his pants (I've repeated this in case it didn't sink in the first time).

Our driver passed the bomb back to me, shaking his head and stating "no". I took the bomb and passing it to Jenk's said "no". Jenks took the bomb, gave it to the Plotter "no", the plotter took it, stating "no" to Crab, who put it back in the rack in front of him and said "no". By this time, the Corp had got up from his prone position on my bed and was now not bemused at us. He decided to vent his fury at our driver, who was a very cheerful chap.

What the fuck are you doing (*"Wat de fok maak jy"*)

We were busy seeing if it was our time Corporal (*"Ons was besig om te sien of dit ons tyd was of nie, Korporaal"*).

If that bomb went off, then all of us could have been blown up (*"As die bom afgegaan het, kon ons almal opgeblaas gewees het"*)!

The corporal did have a point, a HE bomb going off was lethal within 25m.

With a smile on our faces and a knowing look, we all looked at our new Corp and almost in unison said "then it would have been our time" ("*Dan is dit ons tyd*").

Rifleman (retd) S. Benyon

4

Casspir Mine Protected Vehicle

THE AFRICAN MINE TAMER

The Casspir MPV is considered by many to be the father of all the modern enclosed V-shaped monocoque hulled MRAP vehicles which have been developed and deployed by many Western armies. The name Casspir was first coined by Eddie Caromba in May 1979 and is derived from the anagram of SAP and CSIR. The Casspir is also widely used as the vehicle of choice for demining, which involves the removal of anti-personnel and anti-tank landmines, and in humanitarian and peacekeeping operations by the UN around the globe.

DEVELOPMENT

During the mid-1970s the DRU of the CSIR commenced work on a monocoque hull MPV concept. During the same time the SAP requested a vehicle with good off-road capability, mine-protected, field repairable if a mine was detonated, with sufficient armour against small arms fire and which could carry a sufficient number of counter-insurgency personnel. It was to be fielded by the SAP-COIN and SWAPOL-COIN units. The latter SWAPOL-COIN unit was referred to as "Koevoet" (crowbar) and operated in the northern part of SWA against SWAPO. The Casspir also saw extensive use with 101 Battalion and Romeo Mike "Reaction Force" units. From their bases in Angola, SWAPO insurgents would cross the border into SWA and conduct sabotage, intimidation and assassination raids. SWAPO often made use of landmines which were mostly sourced from Warsaw Pact countries such as the USSR. More often than not, innocent civilians would pay the ultimate price.

The first prototype, named *Flossie*, was delivered by CSIR in 1978. The design was somewhat primitive with numerous problems and shortcomings. Made from Bedford truck parts, the vehicle featured a V-bottom armoured monocoque hull design with the suspension modules located on the outside to ease repair and replacement should the module be blown off by a mine. An attempt was made to install a Unimog 352 engine but was unsuccessful. UCCD, which was the biggest importer of Mercedes Benz (MB) parts to South Africa, was approached to assist in improving the design with MB parts. A Mercedes Benz LA1113/42 driveline was fitted successfully in addition to 4x4 truck components which included the engine (OM352), axles, gearbox and transfer box. The first prototype was ready in May 1979, and after a brief trial period, the Casspir was accepted by the SAP who placed an order for 140 vehicles early in 1980. Ultimately, 190 Casspir Mk1 vehicles were manufactured by Henred Fruehauf.

From 1981 production of the Casspir was transferred to TFM Limited who designed the Mk2. On the outside, the Mk1 and Mk2 were very similar, with the latter having the escape hatch located on the left side of the vehicle removed. Additionally, TFM Limited designed a whole range of support vehicles in 1982 based on the Casspir hull. Being so impressed by the vehicle's successful use against SWAPO insurgents, the SADF showed interest as early as 1982/3 and came to incorporate the Casspir Mk2 and Mk3 into the SWATF 101 Battalion and the elite 5 Reconnaissance Regiment, better known as Recces.

The Casspir production companies have changed hands over the past 25 years on a regular basis. For clarity the sequence is as follow: TFM was taken over by Reumech. Reumech, in turn, was taken over by the UK-based Vickers Defence Systems and subsequently renamed Vickers OMC. When Alvis purchased Vickers Defence Systems to become Alvis Vickers, Vickers OMC became Alvis OMC. In 2004, BAE Systems acquired Alvis Vickers, and Alvis OMC was renamed Land Systems OMC. In 2015, the South African defence firm Denel purchased a 75% controlling share in Land Systems OMC which brought the ownership of the Casspir back to South Africa, so to speak. In 2007, some 167 Casspirs were upgraded under Project Gijima. New and improved hull designs

Casspir MK3 APC – AAD 2018. (D. Venter)

Casspir 81mm Mortar weapons platform. (D. Haugh)

Casspir 106 Recoilless gun weapons platform. (D. Haugh)

coupled with the all-important V-shaped armoured underbelly, helps disperse and deflect mine blast energy away from the hull. Making use of commercially available parts reduces its reliance on a specialised logistical train (the process of producing and supplying parts) with the added benefit of decreasing the need for support vehicles for spare parts and specialised maintenance while deployed. The front of the vehicle is strengthened and optimized for bundu bashing. It can travel long distances on road (800km/500mi) without having to refuel and at a comfortable pace of 90km/h (56mph), which arguably makes it one of the most versatile MPVs ever fielded. The Mk3 (and subsequent variants) used by the SADF has a thicker V-shaped hull, 14:00x20 tyres and a different engine. The Mk3 standard also includes structural alterations for improved mobility, with more robust axles.

Mobility

The Casspir's 4x4 configuration was designed for the African battlespace and characterised by its versatility and cross-country capability. As with all wheeled vehicles, it requires less maintenance than their tracked counterparts. It has a ground clearance of 365mm (14.4in) and can ford 1m (3.3ft) of water. The Mk2 is equipped with the ADE 352T six-cylinder turbocharged, water-cooled diesel engine which produces 166hp (124kW) resulting in 15.5hp/t. The engine is located at the front of the vehicle and is coupled to a Mercedes Benz MB G5 five-speed synchromesh manual transmission. It has five forward gears and one reverse. The transfer box is the Mercedes-Benz VG 500-3W. The power is transferred to axles (Mk1 and Mk2 used Mercedes-Benz axles and Mk3 ZF axles) of which the rear has a differential lock.

The Casspir MK2C (I) variant makes use of an upgraded Tata driveline system developed by Denel Mechem in 2010. The power pack of the Mk2C(I) consists of a Tata 697 TC diesel engine that develops 157hp (117kW) at 2,800rpm coupled to a Tata GBS-50 transmission with five forward and one reverse gear as well as a Tata transfer case. The front axles are Tata FA 106 rated at 6,500kg while the rear axles are Tata RA 106 rated at 10t. As with most other South African designed military wheeled vehicles, the Casspir was

have emerged such as the NG2000 and NG2000B. As of 2017, more than 2,800 Casspirs in a number of variants have been produced for the South African and export markets. It is estimated that some 170 are still in service with the SANDF. Among the foreign users are Angola, Benin, Burundi, the Democratic Republic of the Congo, Djibouti, Egypt, Ghana, India, Indonesia, Iraq, Malawi, Mozambique, Namibia, Nepal, Peru, Saudi Arabia, Senegal, Sierra Leone, Tanzania, Uganda and the United States.

DESIGN FEATURES

The Casspir was designed primarily as a mine-resistant APC which could operate in some of the most hostile terrains in the world. The Casspir has several characteristics which have led to its success. It is of 4x4 design coupled with differential lock, making use of four large run-flat tyres which are designed to resist the effects of deflation when punctured. It has a high ground clearance (365mm), which, designed with the challenges of the African Bush in mind. The Casspir is incredibly stable and has excellent off-road mobility due to its simple and innovatively designed suspension and powertrain. It features a semi-elliptic leaf spring (front and rear) which allows for a great degree of deflecting. To improve stability and maximise comfort, check straps were incorporated to counter the axle rebound.

Blesbok – Sandstone Heritage Estate. (D. Venter)

Endurance and logistics

The Casspir has a 200l fuel tank which grants it an operational range of 800km (500mi) via road and 400km (250mi) off-road. It has a road speed of 90km/h (56mph) and a cross-country speed of 28km/h (17mph). A modular design was chosen in order to ease maintenance and reduce the logistical requirement. The Casspir makes use of interchangeable components which are easily accessible. The Casspir also featured a 200/220l water tank which is vital given the expected lengths and conditions the vehicle spends in the field.

Main armament

Although the Casspir is not fitted with weapons as standard, a primary gun mount is sometimes added above the driver's compartment. The armament usually consists of either a 7.62mm or 12.7mm

Duiker – Fuel bowser. (D. Haugh)

MG. During the South African Border War, some Casspirs were fitted with 20mm Hispano cannons originating from retired SAAF fighter planes such as the Spitfire Mk.IX and DE Havilland Vampire jets. Units such as Koevoet made use of captured weapons which included KPV/KPVT 14.5mm HMGs. The co-driver's front window can also be equipped with a machine gun making use of a gimbal mount. Six gun-ports are located on either side of the troop compartment as well as two in the rear doors for close-in defence.

Vehicle layout

The engine and transmission are also located inside the armoured hull to reduce major damage if a mine is detonated. The Casspir has a crew of two which consists of a driver and vehicle commander/gunner and can accommodate 10-12 passengers. The Casspir follows a traditional design with the engine in the front, the crew compartment behind and the troop compartment extending to the rear. The troop compartment has three rectangular bulletproof windows and six firing ports on either side of the hull. Passenger seats face inwards and are equipped with a four-point safety harness. Access to the troop compartment is provided via two air-operated rear doors which can be remotely opened by the driver. The doors are equipped with bulletproof window blocks. The crew compartment roof has an open-top extending down the centre from just behind the driver and crew commander to the rear. During the South African Border War, the roof hatches in the crew and troop compartment were often left open, especially during summer, allowing much-needed air to enter. Early Casspirs had a small fan retrofitted to keep onboard equipment cool. Modern variants are often fitted with air-conditioning units.

Protection

The Casspir can protect its occupants against a triple TM-57 mine blast under any wheel or a double mine blast under the hull. The success of the Casspir as an MPV lies in its narrow V-bottom

Gemsbok – Recovery. (SA Army)

Plofadder – Dedicated mine clearing vehicle. (SA Army)

warfare, Blesbok cargo support, Duiker fuel bowser, Gemsbok recovery vehicle, Plofadder mine clearing, ambulance and vehicle-mounted metal detection system, Groundshout psychological warfare system and law enforcement.

81mm Mortar weapons platform

The 81mm mortar weapons platform is based on the Casspir Mk3 and is a rebuild of an existing vehicle. This version features a fully enclosed crew compartment at the front of the vehicle while the rear mortar compartment offers armour protection on the sides and rear. The sides and rear are fitted with bulletproof windows for better all-round vision. It can carry a total of 192 mortar rounds, stored in ready to use racks with the associated number of charges and fuses. By combining an 81mm mortar with a Casspir, the time into and out of action is reduced and which leads to quicker target engagement and a reduction in the possibility of the mortar weapon's platform being located and neutralized through counter-battery fire. To enhance its tactical flexibility, the mortar can be removed and used in the ground role should it be required or if the vehicle is disabled. A 7.62mm machinegun is mounted on the roof for all-round defence.

106 Recoilless rifle weapons platform

Also based on the Casspir Mk2, rebuilt from an existing vehicle, the 106 Recoilless rifle weapons platform features a fully enclosed crew (front) and troop (middle) compartment with the 106mm M40 recoilless rifle located at the rear. The side and rear panels can be folded down, allowing the gun to be laid on target. A total of twelve 106mm HEAT rounds are carried in a ready to use state. The HEAT round is capable of penetrating 450mm (17.8in) RHA and can be accurately used at a range of 1.1km (0.68mi). To enhance the tactical flexibility of the weapons platform, the gun can be removed and utilised in a ground role should it be required or if the vehicle is disabled. A 7.62mm machinegun is mounted on the roof for all-round defence. There are 32 in operational service with the SANDF.

armoured monocoque hull design which deflects blast energy and debris away from the hull. The fuel tank features a blast-proof cap and is located on the inside of the armoured hull to protect it from mine blasts thereby reducing the chances of a secondary explosion. The hull is rated to protect against 7.62mm NATO and 7.62mm AK-47 Ball.

The Casspir Family

The versatility of the Casspir hull is best understood when evaluating the entire family of combat and support vehicles which have spawned therefrom. South African Motorised Infantry forces field a variety of these vehicles, built on the Mk2 and Mk3 hull, which includes the following variants: 81mm mortar weapons platform, 106 Recoilless rifle weapons platform, artillery fire control, electronic

Artillery fire control

The SANDF has a several artillery fire-control vehicles based on the Casspir. Externally, they are set apart by the additional radio antennas and a large telescopic mast.

Electronic warfare

Casspir Mk3s were converter by the SANDF for electronic warfare use. No public information is available on numbers and capabilities.

Blesbok cargo support vehicle

The Blesbok was a dedicated logistics vehicle used by the COIN units during the South African Border War. Each fighting group of four Casspir MPVs would be allocated one Blesbok cargo support logistics vehicle which would carry ammunition, rations, spares, fuel and camping equipment. This allowed the fighting groups to operate independently for up to a week without resupply. The Blesbok consisted of an armoured two-man driving cab at the front with individual doors for the driver and commander. The cargo area is located at the rear and is equipped with drop sides for easy loading and offloading. It has a carrying capacity of 5t and can also be fitted with a 1,000ℓ (264gal) water or fuel tank. A single 7.62mm BMG can be mounted on the roof as well as in the front left window. A total of 160 vehicles were built for the SAP.

Duiker fuel bowser

The Duiker is a dedicated diesel fuel bowser that consisted of an armoured two-man driving cab at the front with individual doors for the driver and commander and a 3,000ℓ or 5,000ℓ (1,321gal) bowser at the rear. It featured a gravity feed system with an optional electric pump. A single 5.56mm Vector Mini-SS LMG could be mounted on the roof as well as in the front left window. A total of 30 vehicles were built for the SAP.

Gemsbok recovery

The Gemsbok is a dedicated 15t recovery vehicle with an extended armoured five-man driving cab at the front. The cab has an individual door for the driver and commander with an additional side door fitted on the left-hand side. The recovery equipment is located at the rear of the vehicle. The vehicle itself weighs 15.8t. Some 30 Gemsbok were produced for the SAP.

Plofadder

The Plofadder serves as a dedicated mine clearing vehicle. It consists of an armoured two-man driving cab at the front and makes use of a 60AT rocket-propelled mine-clearing system which is slid into the back of the Casspir on rails from where it is launched through the open roof. Rails for loading the containers are carried on the side of the vehicle. The cable drum for the remote-control system to fire the rocket is located on the right side of the vehicle.

Casspir ambulance – Military display, Bloubergstrand. (J. van Zyl)

Groundshout – Psychological warfare system. (G. van Niekerk)

Ambulance

Making use of the standard Casspir, the Casspir ambulance features an armoured two-man driving cab at the front with individual doors for the driver and commander. The rear passenger compartment has been modified to carry two stretcher cases and three seats. Provision was made for storage of standard medical equipment such as a rack for drips. The rear compartment is also fitted with blackout curtains.

MECHEM vehicle mounted metal detection system

Developed by Denel MECHEM, the MVMMDS makes use of a modified Casspir which tows a rubber mat containing the VAMIDS system which detects and marks the location of a landmine with white marking fluid. This system has had wide success in Sudan and Eritrea.

Groundshout psychological warfare system

The Groundshout psychological warfare system variant of the Casspir was used by CSI as early as 1986. It was assigned to 101 Battalion under the command of Cmdt Les Rudman in 1987 near

South African Public Order Police Casspir. (A. Mathey)

Sesspir – Owambo land near Mahnene, Northern Namibia 1988. (A. Swanepoel)

allocated to dedicated public order police units specialising in riot control. The present SAPS Casspir features larger bulletproof windows for increased vision in urban areas with added grills against rocks. The grill for the commander's and driver's windscreen can be pneumatically raised to increase vision. An innovative feature is a front buffer (Bulbar) which can be lowered from inside the vehicle to bulldoze barricades and other obstructions. Additionally, a wire cutter can be mounted on the roof.

Sesspir

The Sesspir was a six-wheel variant (hence the name Ses which is Afrikaans for six) for trials in 1984-85 based on feedback received from SADF troops whose Casspirs lost a front wheel in a landmine detonation which immobilised them during a contact situation. Featuring an extended nose to accommodate the additional front wheels the Sesspir however, made use of the standard Casspir engine. Two Sesspir vehicles were built and issued to 101 Battalion during 1987 for operational trials. One was destroyed during Operation Firewood. It was found that the additional wheels placed too much demand on the standard Casspir engine which needed to push along the front wheels. The remaining Sesspir was converted back to an ordinary Casspir.

Mavingo. The Casspir was equipped with 3600 watts from 4900 watt AEM amps that drove 32 speakers with a 45 volt 100 amp engine-driven alternator using a 36 volt Gates SBS110 battery. The equipment was mounted on a steel chassis which was bolted onto the seat belt bolts. Making use of a hydraulic telescopic boom designed by Skyjacks the speakers could be elevated for broadcast and turned left and right as well as up and down. According to sources, FAPLA was very disturbed by Groundshout, especially those in the trenches on the Lomba who absolutely hated it. Their morale was already low from the constant fighting with the SADF followed at night by screaming animal sounds and armoured vehicle movement emanating from the Groundshout. The system could be heard from as far as 8km (4.9mi). Recently the SANDF have used two refurbished Groundshout vehicles during the COVID-19 pandemic while on patrol to communicate protocol with South Africans.

Law enforcement

As the original user of the Casspir, the SAP maintained a large contingent of Casspirs to maintain civil order during the pre-democratic South Africa. After the first democratic elections in 1994, the SAP was renamed the SAPS. With less need for Casspirs, the SAPS sold a large number of the vehicles. The remainder was

OPERATIONAL HISTORY

During the South African Border War, Casspirs operated by Koevoet would travel in fighting groups of four with a Blesbok (supply, logistics) and Duiker (diesel/fuel) for between 5-7 days covering roughly 600-800km (373-497mi). Each Casspir has a built-in 200ℓ (53gal) water tank, and two spare tyres mounted either side of the lower exterior hull or either side to the rear of the troop compartment.

Since its introduction in 1984 and subsequent evolution variants the Casspir family of APCs formed an integral part of motorised operations by the former SADF during the South African Border War where it was used extensively by motorised infantry of 101 Battalion. 101 Battalion was a quick reaction unit stationed in northern SWA, south of the Angolan border. Making use of the Casspir's mobility and speed they would respond with force to insurgency raids by SWAPO from Angola into SWA. Each team in a company would consist of four Casspirs generally armed with two Hispano Suiza 20mm cannons, six 12.7mm BMGs, four 7.62mm BMGs and four 60mm patrol mortars. Expert Bushman trackers

Africa and exported Casspirs have seen extensive service in the Middle East, especially in Iraq and Afghanistan, where they have saved countless Coalition soldiers' lives.

The Casspirs' use by COIN units during the South African Border War is captured by the author Peter Stiff in his book *Taming the Landmine*.

Mine incidents

The Casspirs primary role was in counterinsurgency missions while protecting its users from landmine blasts. The accompanying statistics show its success in this regard.

Koefoet fighting group Zulu Foxtrot on patrol with Casspirs in Angola in 1984. (J. Durand)

Table 2: Certified Casspir mine incidents

Type of mine	Incidents	Killed	Injured	Personnel
Single mines (6kg [13 lb] TNT)	191	6	167	-
Double mines (12kg [26 lb] TNT)	35	2	69	-
Triple mines (18kg [39 lb] TNT)	1	1	0	-
Four mines (24kg [52 lb] TNT)	2	3	16	-
Total number	229	12	252	2784

would follow the insurgent *spoor* (tracks) while the Casspirs with heavy armament would be a short breath behind to provide direct and overwhelming fire support as soon as contact was made with the insurgents.

The combination of speed, mobility and firepower made the Casspirs exceptionally effective against the insurgents. There were on average 200 contacts during a year with insurgent groups numbering between 5-200 members. 101 Battalion was disbanded in 1991 when SWA gained its independence as Namibia. Casspirs were deployed during the 1998 SADC intervention in Lesotho, which was led by the SANDF. The Casspir has become the face of the UN peacekeeping forces in mine-riddled conflict zones in

CONCLUSION

The Casspir was the first monocoque hull MPV to enter military service during the Cold War and is regarded by military analysts as the grandfather of all subsequent MPV designs. The Casspir set the standard for modern MPV vehicles which later influences MRAPs fielded by the United States of America and most Western nations. For its time, it was one of the best MPVs in the world. The Casspir has left a 35-year legacy, and through continued research and modifications still maintain a defining benchmark against which other wheeled MPV can be measured. The Casspir family of vehicles became the backbone of the SADF motorised battalions and served with distinction during the 26 years South African Border War. Since 1993/94 no production of the Casspir family of vehicles took place for the SANDF. However, an extensive rebuilding programme of old series Casspirs was commissioned as part of Project Gijimain in 2004, with 174 MK2 being refurbished and upgraded to MK3 by 2007. The SANDF has an estimated 370 Casspirs in service primarily assigned to its motorised infantry battalions. There is presently no foreseen replacement for the Casspir in the SANDF. Building on the success of the Casspir, Denel Mechem has introduced a new generation of Casspir originally designated as Mk4 and re-branded as the Casspir NG2000 series of vehicles which is a complete improvement on the original using new production techniques.

5

G6 Rhino Self-Propelled Howitzer-Vehicle

THE AFRICAN LONG RANGE BRAWLER

The G6 is named after the indigenous African Rhinoceros, an animal which is massive in size and extremely powerful stationary and even more so when charging a threat. Armed with a long protruding horn on its snout, a rhino can devastate any attacker. Unlike its animal namesake, the G6 Rhino is agile for its bulk. The G6 was planned at the height of the Cold War by South Africa to replace its aging WW2 artillery pieces and to counter Eastern Bloc-supplied artillery used by the MPLA and FAPLA. The G6 is a three-axle, six-wheeled self-propelled howitzer which forms the backbone of the SANDF artillery arm who can field 43 vehicles.

DEVELOPMENT

During the 1960s and 1970s, the SADF still employed WW2 artillery such as the 88mm quick-firing gun (25-pounder) which was designated G1, 140mm howitzers designated G2 and the Sexton self-propelled artillery piece, to name a few. The SADF needed to upgrade its artillery and the requirement to modernise their inventory was set in 1968 and formalised during 1973. South Africa also obtained several American made M1 155mm towed howitzers designated as G3, which were used to develop gun drills, doctrine and logistics for the G5-45 155mm advanced long-range field artillery system (known as the Leopard).

Project Sherbett III began in 1976, led by the SRC under the famous Dr Gerald Bull. The contract for the G6 hull and drive train was awarded to Sandock Austral, and their design team did most of the work while LEW designed the G6 turret and gun control system. The integration of the G5-45 155mm advanced long-range field artillery gun control system into a turret was allocated to Kentron. ESD was tasked with the development of the rammer control system (loading system) while Naschem was responsible for

G6-45 – AAD 2018. (S Tegner)

G6-45 – Public display. (R. Fouche)

ammunition sub-systems. The G6 was subsequently armed with the same gun as the G5-45 and designated as the G6-45.

The development of the G6 self-propelled gun-howitzer began in earnest during 1979 at ARMSCOR under Project Zenula. The first advanced prototype was completed in October 1981, and by 1987 four G6 vehicles had been built and were pressed into service in the same year during the South African Border War. One G6 suffered an engine failure due to a hole in the engine pump from a bolt that fell in during a compressor change. It was subsequently towed to Mavinga

G6-45 – Front nose projectile storage racks. (D. Venter)

while a replacement engine was flown in. Three days later, after the new engine was installed, the vehicle set out to join the other three G6 already deployed in the bush. All four vehicles returned to South Africa under their own power near mid-December 1987.

Full-scale production began in 1988 and lasted until 1994. A modernisation program codename Project Vasvat was implemented in 1993 to ensure all G6s had the same equipment and characteristics. A variant of the G6 known as the H45 is operated by Oman (24) and United Arab Emirates (78). Denel Land Systems has continued to upgrade the G6 platform and unveiled the G6-52 in 2003, showcasing improved key features, such as mobility, speed, range, accuracy, ease of operation, rate of fire, full protection against counter-battery fire and adaptability. Two variants of the G6-52 were produced, one with a standard 23ℓ (6gal) chamber and the other with a larger 25ℓ (6.6gal)chamber identified by the ER designation.

At the time of writing 15 G6-45s are undergoing an upgrade under Project Muhali to replace obsolete items. The project is set to be completed in June 2021. Also Project Topstar is set to upgrade the gun laying and navigation systems of the G6-45.

DESIGN FEATURES

The G6 sports a low-silhouetted 6x6 wheeled hull designed and optimised for the distances and terrain it would operate on, which can be described as some of the most hostile in the world. The G6 is characterised by its six massive 21:00x25 wheels, fast setup time, bush breaking ability and versatility as a howitzer platform. In skilled hands, during the South African Border War, the G6 proved itself more than capable

of inflicting heavy losses. The G5 was designed with a secondary self-defensive direct anti-tank role in mind. It is thought that it could defeat any composite armoured MBT of the time and the same is true for the G6. It came as a nasty surprise to FAPLA, as it dominated the battlespace by outshooting, outranging and outmanoeuvring enemy artillery.

Mobility

The long distances in Southern Africa and low force density necessitated a vehicle that could operate under its own power. The wheeled configuration subsequently granted the G6 operational mobility, as it does not require heavy transport or trains to reach its destination in line with SADF doctrine for mobile warfare.

G6-45 – Outside fighting compartment, artillery projectile and charges storage racks in rear of hull. At the rear of turret is the APU and air-conditioning housing. On the right rear corner is the entry and exit door to the turret interior fighting compartment. AAD 2012. (S. Tegner)

G6-45 – Powerpack right side with gearbox, air intake (right) and fuel tank (left) visible. (D. Venter)

G6-45 – Powerpack left side with engine and fuel tank visible. (D. Venter)

offers excellent operational and tactical mobility. Torsion bar suspension units with hydraulic shock dampers and bump stops are located on all six wheels. The steering is hydraulically assisted.

The rear of the turret bustle contains a Deutz F2L511 air-cooled two-cylinder four-stroke diesel engine which produces 45hp (34kW). There is also an APU with which the batteries are recharged and air-conditioning units are powered for crew comfort. The driver's compartment air-conditioning is powered by the main engine. The G6-52 features an upgraded 50hp (37kW) turret-mounted APU.

The G6 electrical system consists of two 24-volt batteries that provide 175-ampere-hour for the hull while four 12-volt batteries provide 390-ampere-hour for the turret.

Endurance and Logistics

The G6 is equipped with two fuel tanks on either side of the midsection of the hull with a combined capacity of 700ℓ (185gal) giving it an operational road range of 700km (435mi) and 350km (218mi) cross-country, allowing flexible force movement in conjunction with mechanised formations. Although the G6 can reach a road speed of 85km/h (53mph), its recommended cruising speed is 70km/h (44mph), while cross-country speed of between 30-40km/h (19-25mph) can be reached, terrain dependant.

The G6 has a 150ℓ (40gal) drinking water tank which is accessible via a tap located at the rear of the vehicle, underneath the hull.

As proven during combat operations during the South African Border War and per SADF/SANDF doctrine, the G6 can operate on long missions cross-country over rugged and variable terrain, bush-break new routes and provide superior long-distance artillery support for nearly a month with very little technical and logistical support. Improvements made to the G6-52 chassis have simplified maintenance and lengthened periods between service intervals.

Vehicle layout

The G6 is manned by a crew of six consisting of a commander, layer, breech operator, loader, ammunition handler, and driver. During an engagement, the ammunition handler and driver prepare and load the ammo from the outside rear to the loader inside the turret.

The driver's compartment is located at the front-centre of the vehicle between the two front wheel wells. The driver has day

The vehicle makes use of a central tyre-inflation system which controls the six-run flat radial tire configuration. The tyres can be pressurised according to either soft, medium or hard terrain whilst on the move. All wheels are equipped with hydro-pneumatic drum brakes.

The G6 can lose a rear or middle wheel and still remain manoeuvrable off-road. Such advantages, however, come at a cost. In order for wheeled vehicles (above 10t) to achieve acceptable cross-country mobility, overall large size and high levels of mechanical complexity are required when compared to tracked counterparts.

The engine and gearbox are mounted on a subframe, located between the driver's compartment and the fighting compartment. The G6 makes use of a Magirus Deutz BF12L513 FC V12 air-cooled diesel engine which produces 550hp (11.9hp/t). This allows the vehicle to acceleration from 0-30km/h (0-19mph) in 12 seconds.

The G6 makes use of a Denel Vehicle Systems automatic gearbox (RENK family of gearboxes) with six forward and one reverse gear ratios and can be manually overridden if the need arises. The vehicle features a permanent six-wheeled drive configuration with selectable longitudinal and differential locks. This configuration night viewing capabilities and an excellent 180-degree field-of-view through three large bulletproof glass windows. During battle, the driver can activate an armoured shield which pops-up and covers the front window for extra protection. When the armoured shield is activated, the driver uses a day periscope with a view of the front. Located behind the driver is the gearbox and engine (power pack) and the driver can only enter and exit the vehicle through a roof hatch located above his seat. The driver's station contains a comprehensive engine monitoring system.

The turret is mounted at the rear of the vehicle hull, above the two rear axles and is manned by the commander, layer, breech operator and loader. It features several viewing ports, a gyro laying sight for indirect fire and telescope for direct firing. The commander and breech operator are located on the right side of the ordinance while the layer and loader are seated on the left. The commander's station has basic driving controls from where he can switch off the engine and apply an emergency brake to stop the vehicle. He also has access to a cupola which offers 360-degree viewing and a roof hatch.

A secondary air defence 12.7mm or 7.62mm BMG for close defence can be mounted on the left cupola. The primary function of the 12.7mm BMG is to engage low flying enemy aircraft, lightly skinned armoured vehicles and suppress enemy infantry. Up to 2,000 rounds of 7.62mm or 1,000 rounds of 12.7mm ammunition can be carried aboard.

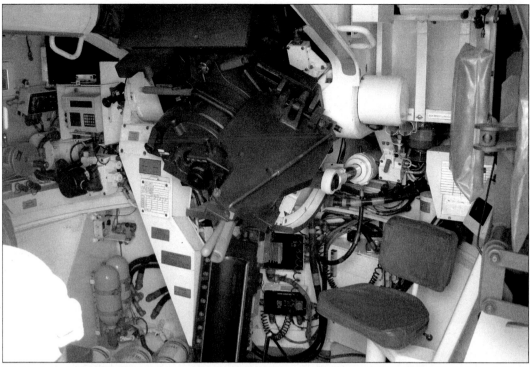

G6-45 – Forward interior of turret fighting compartment. The gunner's station is at the far left with the breech block visible in the middle. AAD 2012. (S. Tegner)

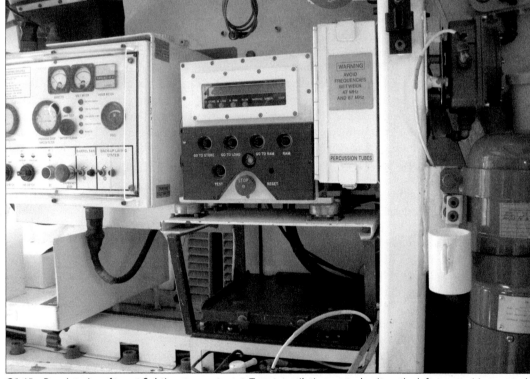

G6-45 – Rear interior of turret fighting compartment. Turret ventilation control unit on the left, ammunition control on the right. Below is the radio station. AAD 2012. (S. Tegner)

The rear-right of the turret features a hatch for crew access. A dedicated hatch for ammunition loading from outside is located at the rear-centre of the turret, near the floor.

One bank of four 81mm electrically operated smoke grenade launchers is located on either side of the front of the turret. The turret also has five firing ports (two left, two right and one rear) should the crew need to use their R4 rifles for close-in defence.

Main armament

The G6's primary armament is a 155mm 45-calibre main gun while the G6-52 uses a longer 155mm 52-calibre main gun. Much of the early long-distance shooting success of the G6 was due to its blast chamber having a volume of 23ℓ (6gal), compared to the standard international 21ℓ (5.5gal). The G6-52 also features a 23ℓ (6gal) blast chamber while the G6-52 ER has a 25ℓ (6.6gal) chamber.

The G6's 155mm gun uses a single-baffle muzzle brake and an upgraded hydro-pneumatic recoil system and rammer which grants a sustained three rounds a minute rate of fire. The G6-52 features a barrel cooling fan system, a modified multi-baffle design, and a new

G6-SPAAM – DEXA 1992. (J. Botha)

Fire control system

The FCC of the G6 is indirect, as targeting data originates from forward observers, who pass it on through the ATES to a fire control post before finally being transmitted to the individual G6 LMS via frequency-hopping VHF radio.

The G6 layer can only aim the ordinance via a telescopic sight for direct-fire missions while the G6-52 makes use of an automatic gun-laying system. The G6-52 features an automatic fire-control system (AS2000) which includes an automatic gun laying and navigation system (FIN 3110 RLG) designed by DLS. The G6-52 features a new LMS computer and integrates the fire control computer system, GPS receiver and the ring laser gyroscope with a touchscreen display and DLS sensors. This enables the G6-52 to launch multiple round simultaneous impact fire; this involves the firing of several shots at different arcs towards a target so that they impact at the same time, which ensures maximum surprise as shells impact their target at the same time. This can be done up to a maximum range of 50km (31mi).

Although the G6 is capable of firing from a wheeled stance, it is equipped with four hydraulically-operated stabiliser legs; two of which are located between the first and second wheel pairs and two located behind the rear wheels. These can be deployed for optimal stability. The G6 can deploy to fire in under one minute and can be mobile again in the same time, which allows for quick 'shoot and scoot' tactics, making it challenging to locate, target, and hit with counter-battery fire.

Protection

The G6 features an all-welded steel alloy armour which provides protection from small arms fire, ballistic fragments and explosive concussion across the whole chassis. The frontal arc of the vehicle and turret offers protection from 20mm armour piercing rounds. The turret has several firing ports for the crew's personal weapons. As with most South African produced military vehicles, the chassis is mine-protected, with the floor of the vehicle being double layered for improved protection. This allows the G6 to withstand three TM57 anti-tank landmine explosions. The G6 incorporates an overpressure biological and chemical protection system while the G6-52 offers full NBC protection system. In case of an on-board fire, the G6 is equipped with an automatic fire-extinguishing system.

G6 SPAAM

When the Rooikat ZA-35 SPAAG and SPAAM (see Chapter 11) was cancelled, and attempt was made to revive the project using a mock-up based on a G6 platform with a wooden turret structure. It served as a demonstrator of possibilities to breech the gap between existing technologies an potential solutions, which culminated in a paper study. No ammunition was produced however the SAHV-3 would have most certainly found its way to the intended role if the project went ahead.

rammer which increases the rate of fire to six rounds per minute. The G6 breech mechanism features an interrupted screw stepped-thread while the G6-52 makes use of a combination swingblock with mushroom head and sliding block. The elevation is maxed at +75 and -5 degrees with a traverse of maximum 40 degrees either left or right horizontally from the centre.

The G6 carries 39 – 41 projectiles, 50 charges, 60 primers and 39 fuses with an additional 18 backup fuses. A total of 19 projectiles are carried inside the turret fighting compartment for emergency use only, while eight projectiles are stored on either side of the nose of the vehicle. Another four projectiles and the majority of the charges are stored in exterior rear compartments of the hull in a special blast-out magazine and are used first when in a stationary firing position. The G6-52 makes use of a carousel with 40 projectiles and 40 charges.

All ammunition used by the G6 was developed in South Africa and supplied by Rheinmetall Denel Munitions. The G6 can fire all standard NATO 155mm ammunition as well as the M1 series ERFB and ERF-BB ammunition.

The G6 makes use of the M64 MCS, the latter achieving a velocity of 909m/s (2982f/s) HE-BB or 911m/s (2989f/s) for the HE. Of note is the M9703 V-LAP which combines base-bleed and rocket motor technology developed under Project Assegai. Previously the G6-52 ER had achieved a range of 70km (43.5mi) by combining the M64 MCS and V-LAP. As of November 2019, the bar has been raised when a G6-52 ER fired an RDM M9703 V-LAP with an M64 Zone six charge, that reached 76.3km (47.4mi).

Table 3: G6 variants and ammunition firing ranges			
Ammunition	G6-45	G6-52	G6-52 ER
HE without base bleed	30km (18.6mi)	-	-
HE with base bleed	40.5km (25.2mi)	42km (26mi)	50km (31mi)
HE with V-LAP	52.5km (32.6mi)	58km (36mi)	76.2km (47.4mi)

Note: All firing ranges except V-Lap/G6-52 are at sea level.

OPERATIONAL HISTORY

South African G6s have only ever been used operationally during the South African Border War and subsequently proved its combat capability. The G6 fielded by UAE armed forces in Yemen has been actively used in its conflict since August 2015.

CONCLUSION

Few would disagree that the G6 was ahead of its time when it was first fielded in 1987. The SANDF actively operates nine G6 vehicles while the remaining 34 are in preservation storage during peacetime. Characterised by its impressive fire range, mobility, speed, accuracy and endurance, it remains at the front of the pack when compared to other wheeled and tracked self-propelled howitzer vehicles. The original objectives of long-range fire, speed, mobility, flexibility, and easy logistics are complemented by the G6's overall crew protection. Through continued upgrades, the G6 can remain a force to be reckoned with in the field of self-propelled howitzer vehicles in the foreseeable future.

G6 – Trials at Riemvasmaak, South Africa 1987. (H.R. Smith)

A soldier's account with the G6 – Trial and test

During my compulsory two-year army stint with the Artillery Corps during 1986/87, I was very fortunate to get the opportunity to be exposed to the new weapon being developed for the artillery, namely the G6 Rhino but commonly called just the G6. It so happened that during 1987 the weapon development had reached a point where there was now four PPM – each one was different in certain small ways, but generally, they all performed the same task – that was ready for further testing also known as Proofs or "*Proewe*".

ARMSCOR/Denel approached the artillery unit, and somehow our battery 1 Med was chosen, and the "*Proewe*" (trial) team was put together. I don't recall if we were asked to volunteer to be part of it or whether we were instructed: "you and you and you" are going on G6 "*Proewe*", in the army, this was also classified as volunteering, so it made no difference.

The four preproduction models were driven from the factory to the 10 Art Brigade Base in Potchefstroom, and then all necessary support vehicles were sourced to accompany the G6s. Ammo Kwêvoël 100's with trailers, Ratels etc.

After much organising and getting supplies etc. we left the "*comforts*" of our base and hit the road with these colossal machines and the fleet of support vehicles onto the South African roads. The look on public vehicle drivers' faces was indeed a sight to see, and I'm sure there were a few accidents caused by people gawking at these monstrous machines and the ammo trucks etc.

I do not recall [the] exact places we travelled, but it was basically to test the whole concept of creating a very fast (90kph [56mi]) and mobile artillery weapon. It was quite capable of getting around 120kph (75mph) on roads which was a first of its kind worldwide. Yes, we already had the G5 which is self-propelled in a sense, but that is only for very short distances and basically in the battle area — the G5 still has to be towed in the event you need to get to a battle area 20/50/100/1,000km (12/31/62/621mi) away as was our scenario and yes there are other tracked artillery guns in the world, but these also had to be towed to the battle zone if it is/was any distance. The G6 overcame this need for towing and with a fuel tank range of 700kms, in my opinion, it is still one of the most advanced artillery weapons in the world.

We camped alongside the road in many places and made our way up through Namibia (then SWA) doing all sorts of tests, and we had a team of engineers "*tiffies*" from Denel along with us as well as SADF "*tiffies*" all monitoring performance of the vehicles etc. We spent some time in the Okavango swamps doing tests in swampy conditions and recovery methods of vehicles. Here we used the Mack Recovery aka "*Wit Hings*" (White Stallion) (except ours was painted nutria colours) as well as a MAN 8X8 that we were also testing as a possible replacement for the SAMIL/Kwêvoël gun tractors. We called it ET as it was a strange-looking but exceptionally useful vehicle indeed.

Daily we were performing a different test and having competitions between the crews as to which crew can change a wheel the fastest etc.— all precious learning lessons — and the capabilities of the vehicle under different circumstances.

From SWA we made our way down to a place called Riemvasmaak, which is a railway station/yard bordering onto the Lohatla shooting range, and this is desert country. Here we performed more tests as well as numerous shooting exercises, testing the guns and sights etc. This entire "*Proewe*" lasted roughly three months and was fascinating and exciting learning about the new weapon. Once the boffins were satisfied, we returned to Potchefstroom, and the G6s went back to Pretoria to the factory. This all took place roughly May; June; July 1987.

Day to day life carried on in camp, and then the call came around the middle of October that a battery [8 guns] of G5s had to be taken to Angola, and so off I went on the road again with the convoy of G5s into Angola. Basically, it's a 5-day journey with such a big convoy of vehicles consisting of 8 gun tractors with guns; eight ammo trucks; Ratels; Buffels etc. I think there were 24 vehicles in total.

G6 – During Operation Moduler in Angola, 1987. (H.R. Smith)

If memory serves me correctly, we crossed into Angola on a Wednesday with the G5s and arrived at Masvinga [often spelt Mavinga] which was the SADF *"deurgangskamp"* (transit camp) around midday. Shortly after arriving a radio message came through stating that four other drivers who were part of the G6 *"Proewe"* and I were being airlifted by chopper at 17h00 and flying back to fetch the G6s.

[There was a] mad scramble hand over vehicles and equipment and much excitement waiting for the chopper and [at] 17h00 the chopper could be heard coming in. We scramble on board, and the eggbeaters start a high pitch whine and up you go into the air — treetops flying out was pretty exciting, and we landed 'n transferred onto a *"Flossie"* (C-130 transport plane) and back in the air to Waterkloof Air Force base in Pretoria. We slept at the airport and then picked up the G6s and went back to Potchefstroom on Thursday. Friday morning planning and packing of vehicles were organised, and I think we either left on the Monday or Tuesday back up to Angola arriving at 61 Mech five days later. Our formation was so significant we had to camp outside 61 Base Workshop — four G6s; four Kwêvoël ammo trucks; Ratels, Water tanker; Diesel Tanker; SAMIL 20 ambulance; SAMIL 20 signals truck.

After three or four days outside 61 Mech we went into Angola. Shortly after, one of the G6s experienced mechanical problems, and we towed it through to Mavinga. The other three G6s went operational whilst a new engine and gearbox were flown in, and the *"tiffies"* undertook an engine change in the bush. The "wounded" G6 then joined the other three after its transplant, and the four G6s joined the expeditionary troops of the 4 SAI. Operating independently as a battery, we bombarded strategic MPLA and FAPLA military targets. Of note is the one instance where an airfield near Cuito Cuanavale was targeted. With Special Forces (Recces) serving as forward observers, accurate fire missions were given which allowed us to destroy four Angolan MIG-21s while they were taxiing for take-off. Subsequently, the MPLA was forced to withdraw their aeroplanes to airfields further away and out of the G6 fire range. The end result was that MPLA aircraft had to fly further to execute their aerial mission and subsequently couldn't spend as much time searching for targets.

The myths surrounding the G6 getting stuck and battling in the sand etc. are ABSOLUTE NONSENSE. Not once did we get stuck or have difficulties. Yes, it was harder to drive due to the width of the wheel track in comparison to the conventional tracks one purely got your wheels into, and the vehicle followed the tracks. With the immense power and size of the wheels, the G6 had to break its own tracks which it did with ease. To my knowledge, we never experienced one puncture or flat tyre during our movements in Angola, but yes we had one flat on our way back to SA after leaving Angola.

The performance of the vehicle itself, as well as the performance of the gun, exceeded everyone's expectations and a profound bond was formed amongst us few that were privileged to be the "Guinea Pigs" on this formidable weapon.

The engineering and design of this weapon are remarkable and very user friendly for the gun crew and driver. Once the G6 went into proper production, there have been further improvements and additions as technology has advanced. Unfortunately, I am not informed enough to elaborate or go into detail on these upgrades. I'm just fortunate to have been at the right place at the right time and privileged to have served on that very first G6s.

Lance Bombardier (retd) H.R. Smith

6
Bateleur Multiple Rocket Launcher

THE AFRICAN BIRD OF PREY

The Bateleur FV2 takes its name from a mid-sized eagle native to the open savannah and woodlands of Sub-Saharan Africa. The MRL is aptly named as it was built to operate in the same environment. The Bateleur is a true African born MRL, adapted for the African battlespace and the lessons learned from the South African Border War. The Bateleur was planned in 1983 to replace its smaller predecessor the Visarend (Fish Eagle) FV1. The Bateleur's role was to provide the SADF with first strike capabilities in support of its artillery philosophy as set out in 1974.

DEVELOPMENT

The development of a South African MRL was already underway in 1974 under Project Furrow at the CSIR which led to the Visarend. The SADF was well aware of the capability and danger of the Soviet BM-21 Grad MRL. The BM-21 can fire its 122mm rockets to 20km (12.3mi) which was further than most South African artillery systems at the time and can saturate a football field-sized area with HE rockets within seconds whereas an entire artillery battery of eight guns would be needed to achieve the same effect in the same time frame. The Visarend with its 127mm (5in) rockets would be able to outrange its Soviet counterpart by 12km (7.5mi) due to its better-developed rocket motor. 127mm (5in) was selected as Kentron (later Denel Somchem) at that stage were using the same diameter for their V3 air to air missile. This allowed development with only a few modifications. The conflict steadily escalated as newer Soviet equipment found its way to Angola. The Visarend played a crucial role in several SADF operations such as Operation Protea, Alpha Centauri and Moduler. It was, however, not robust enough for the demands placed on it by the rough terrain and offered no

protection against the ever-present threat of landmines. A more suitable vehicle was required with improved mobility, protection, and increased payload.

Work on the Bateleur initially called the Visarend FV2 began in the mid-1980s under Project Canton and ended in 1986. Somchem was responsible for the Bateleur's development and Denel and ARMSCOR provided technical assistance as needed. The first vehicles were ready to be fielded just as the war came to a close in 1989. The Bateleur is only in service with the SANDF and four of the 25 Bateleurs produced are in preservation storage. At the time of writing the Bateleur is undergoing an upgrade of its rocket laying and navigation systems under Project Topstar.

DESIGN FEATURES

The design, development, and production of the Bateleur were undertaken to improve on the shortcomings of the Visarend which included inadequate protection and lack of mobility over rough terrain. The Bateleur is a three-axle, 6x6 all-wheel drive, 40-tube MRL, based on the robust SAMIL Kwêvoël 100 Withings mine-protected body, which itself was a proven system. The body is V-shaped to deflect mine blasts under the hull away from the crew cabin.

The primary purpose of the Bateleur is to destroy HVT and HIT, which include counterbattery strikes against enemy artillery and air defence emplacements.

Mobility

The Bateleur is a six-wheel configuration offering more reliability and requiring less maintenance than a tracked vehicle. The Bateleur makes use of a ZF 56-65 synchromesh gearbox with a gear selection

Bateleur FV2 – AAD 2018. (D. Venter)

Visarend FV1– Side view, Klipdrif School of Artillery. (D. Venter)

Bateleur FV2 – Rear view, AAD 2018. (D. Venter)

makes use of a WITHINGS suspension and has 355mm (13.9in) of ground clearance.

Endurance and logistics

To facilitate strategic mobility, the Bateleur has two 200ℓ (52.8gal) diesel fuel tanks which give it an effective range of 1,000km (621mi) on road, 500km (310mi) off-road and 250km (155mi) over-sand. It is also fitted with a 200ℓ (52.8gal) water tank underneath the crew compartment. The crew can access the water via a tap located above the front left wheel. The rear launcher carries 40x127mm (5in) rockets in launch tubes. Rockets are supplied by a SAMIL Kwêvoël 100 ammunition truck carrying 96 rockets and personnel who assist with the reloading process.

Vehicle layout

The Bateleur can be divided into two parts, namely the vehicle which consists of the body, crew cabin and drivetrain, and secondly the weapon system consisting of the mounting, cradle and tube pack which includes the sighting and laying system stabilisers. The engine is located at the front of the vehicle with the raised crew cabin behind it, the length of which is built on a V-shaped hull. The engine features a trapezoidal ventilation grid at the front of the hood and beneath it is a forward-facing V-shaped bumper to assist in bundu bashing. The crew cabin is rectangular in shape with two forward-facing rectangular windows. On either side of the cabin are two armoured entry and exit doors each with a rectangular bulletproof window. The roof is armoured and protects against medium artillery fragments. This setup provides all-round protection against small-arms fire, and the V-shaped hull protects the crew from mine blast underneath the hull. Access to either side of the crew cabin doors is via a chain ladder. At the rear of the vehicle hydraulically operated stabiliser legs are deployed when the launcher is to be fired.

The driver station (Bombardier/Lance Bombardier) is located on the forward right side of the cabin with the crew commander (Sergeant) seated on the forward left. Behind them are three seats with the Layer (Lance Bombardier) seated behind the driver, 2IC

range of eight forward and one reverse. The engine is a type FIOL 413 V10 air-cooled 4-stroke Deutz diesel with direct injection which produces 268hp (200kW) at 2,650rpm. This provides a 12.5hp/t power to weight ratio which is more than adequate for its role as an MRL operating behind forward elements.

The Bateleur can achieve a maximum road speed of 90km/h (56mph), and 30km/h (18.6mph) off-road. It can ford 1.2m (3.9ft) of water without preparation and can cross a 0.5m (19.7in) ditch at a crawl. The driver's task eased by a power steering system, while acceleration and braking are done via foot pedals. The vehicle

(Bombardier) in the centre and ammunition loader and gunner (Lance Bombardier) on the left.

The vehicle commander is responsible for communication via the AS2000 command system. The driver station has a range of mobility options depending on terrain type from a panel to his front left and when not driving, he assists with the reloading of rockets. The layer is responsible for laying and orientating the launcher, while the bombardier mans the roof-mounted 7.62mm BMG while in the crew cabin.

Main armament

The launcher carries 40x127mm (5in) rockets in two packs of 5x4 launcher tubes. Rockets are fired in 0.5-second intervals with a full rocket salvo lasting 20 seconds. The launcher is electro-hydraulically operated via a joystick and can elevate to a maximum of 50 degrees and traverse 90 degrees left and 19 degrees right dependant on the elevation. At sea level, the minimum range of the standard 127mm (5in) rockets is 7.5km (4.7mi) with a large drag ring, and maximum range of 22.5km (13.9mi) with no drag ring. Experimental long-range 127mm (5in) rockets have been tested which have a firing range of 37km (22.9mi). A standard HE-Frag rocket is 2.95m (9.67ft) long, weighs 62kg (137lb) and contains 8,500 5.5mm (0.21in) steel balls cast in a resin sleeve filled with an RDX/TNT mix which can be set to detonate either on direct contact or with a proximity fuse depending on the tactical requirements and nature of the target. Six Bateleurs firing ten rockets each will hit a target area of 350m x 250m (383yd x 273yd) and deliver 516,000 high-velocity steel balls (5.9 balls per m²) in a space of five

Bateleur FV2 – Front view, AAD 2012. (D. Venter)

Bateleur FV2 – Drivers compartment, AAD 2018. (D. Venter)

Table 4: Bateleur firing range

127mm (5in) rocket	No drag ring	Small drag ring	Medium drag ring	Large drag ring
Standard	12-22.5km (7.5-13.9mi)	9-15km (5.6-9.3mi)	8-11.5km (4.9-7.1mi)	7-9.5km (4.3-5.9mi)
Extended range	19.6-37km (12.2-22.9mi)	Unknown	Unknown	Unknown

Note: All firing ranges are at sea level.

seconds. Such devastation would be lethal to all unarmoured targets.

The launcher is integrated into the South African developed SAATES which address tactical, terminal and technical fire control as well as individual launcher control through the appropriate hardware and software with integrated digital communication. The selection of rockets, sequence, and arming of the rockets to be fired is selected from a panel located on the dashboard.

At the rear of the vehicle, behind the launcher and body, is a platform that can slide out and provides an elevated position to handle and load the rockets from. Loading the launcher simply

Bateleur FV2 – 127mm (5in) rocket, AAD 2018. (D. Venter)

Bateleur FV2 – firing at Potchefstroom artillery open day. (H. Kotze)

the applicable artillery tactical HQ. Orders are given for the launcher(s) to move to a loading area where it is loaded while the firing position is reconnoitred and prepared. The launcher(s) moves to the firing position where they are accurately orientated on a selected bearing which is typically the centre of the target area. The ATES computer in the FCP determines the bearing and range to the target and then computes the ballistic corrections required to compensate for the existing non-standard conditions. The firing data is transmitted to the launcher(s) in the form of FO which details the bearing and elevation at which the pack is to be laid as well as the drag ring confirmation, the number of rounds and the time on target. After firing, the launcher(s) vacate the firing position (shoot and scoot) to avoid the danger of being spotted by the enemy due to the characteristic launch signature of any MRL system.

Protection

The crew cabin is protected all round from 7.62mm fire, and the roof is rated against medium fragmentation. The V-shaped hull has been tested and proven against three TM-57 landmines or the equivalent of 19kg (42lb) of TNT under the crew cabin.

requires the sliding of a rocket into each of the 40 tubes and it takes between 15 and 20 minutes to reload the launcher. A well-trained crew can be in and out of action in three minutes. For close-up protection, the vehicle can be equipped with a 7.62mm BMG which can be mounted on the roof of the crew cabin.

Fire control system

After a target(s) has been acquired by the appropriate target acquisition resource and analysed, the decision to engage is taken at

CONCLUSION

The Bateleur fulfils a niche role in the SANDF as a medium MRL. It was built according to the same fundamental principles as other wheeled South African military vehicles which places emphasis on long-range fire, speed, mobility, flexibility, and simple logistics. Although the Bateleur has not yet been used in anger, the firepower of the MRL is devastating.

ELAND 90 Mk7 specifications

Crew	3	Gradient (%)	51
Combat weight (t)	6	Trench (m)	0.5
Power-to-weight ratio (hp/t)	14.5	Engine power output (hp)	87
Length (m)	4.04	Number of forward gears	6
Width (m)	2.01	Number of reverse gears	1
Height (m)	2.5	Main weapon calibre (mm)	90
Max. road speed (km/h)	90	Auxiliary gun calibre (mm) x2	7.62
Fuel capacity (ℓ)	142	Ammunition for main weapon	29
Max. road range (km)	450	Ammunition for the auxiliary gun	3,800

ELAND 60 Mk7 specifications

Crew	3	Gradient (%)	51
Combat weight (t)	5.32	Trench (m)	0.5
Power-to-weight ratio (hp/t)	16.4	Engine power output (hp)	87
Length (m)	4.04	Number of forward gears	6
Width (m)	2.01	Number of reverse gears	1
Height (m)	1.88	Main weapon calibre (mm)	60
Max. road speed (km/h)	90	Auxiliary gun calibre (mm) x2	7.62
Fuel capacity (ℓ)	142	Ammunition for main weapon	56
Max. road range (km)	450	Ammunition for the auxiliary gun	2,400

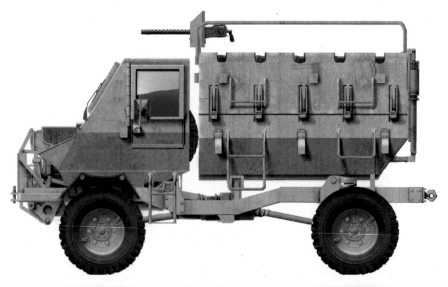

BUFFEL specifications

Crew	1+10	Gradient (%)	60
Combat weight (t)	6.1	Trench (m)	1.2
Power-to-weight ratio (hp/t)	20.4	Engine power output (hp)	125
Length (m)	5.10	Number of forward gears	8
Width (m)	2.05	Number of reverse gears	4
Height (m)	2.96	Main weapon calibre (mm) x2	7.62
Max. road speed (km/h)	96	Auxiliary gun calibre (mm)	-
Fuel capacity (ℓ)	200	Ammunition for main weapon	1,000
Max. road range (km)	1,000	Ammunition for the auxiliary gun	-

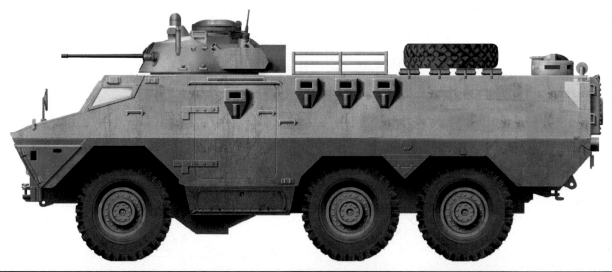

Ratel 12.7 Mk3 specifications

Crew	3 + 6	Gradient (%)	60
Combat weight (t)	18.9	Trench (m)	1.15
Power-to-weight ratio (hp/t)	14.9	Engine power output (hp)	282
Length (m)	7.2	Number of forward gears	6
Width (m)	2.7	Number of reverse gears	2
Height (m)	2.89	Main weapon calibre (mm)	12.7
Max. road speed (km/h)	105	Auxiliary gun calibre (mm) x3	7.62
Fuel capacity (ℓ)	480	Ammunition for main weapon	300
Max. road range (km)	1,000	Ammunition for the auxiliary gun	3,000

Ratel 20 Mk3 specifications

Crew	3 + 8-11	Gradient (%)	60
Combat weight (t)	18.9	Trench (m)	1.15
Power-to-weight ratio (hp/t)	14.9	Engine power output (hp)	282
Length (m)	7.21	Number of forward gears	6
Width (m)	2.70	Number of reverse gears	2
Height (m)	2.94	Main weapon calibre (mm)	20
Max. road speed (km/h)	105	Auxiliary gun calibre (mm) x3	7.62
Fuel capacity (ℓ)	480	Ammunition for main weapon	1,200
Max. road range (km)	1,000	Ammunition for the auxiliary gun	6,000

Ratel 60 Mk3 specifications

Crew	3+7	Gradient (%)	60
Combat weight (t)	18.9	Trench (m)	1.15
Power-to-weight ratio (hp/t)	14.9	Engine power output (hp)	282
Length (m)	7.2	Number of forward gears	6
Width (m)	2.7	Number of reverse gears	2
Height (m)	2.89	Main weapon calibre (mm)	60
Max. road speed (km/h)	105	Auxiliary gun calibre (mm) x3	7.62
Fuel capacity (ℓ)	480	Ammunition for main weapon	45
Max. road range (km)	1,000	Ammunition for the auxiliary gun	6,000

Ratel 90 Mk3 specifications

Crew	3+6	Gradient (%)	60
Combat weight (t)	20	Trench (m)	1.15
Power-to-weight ratio (hp/t)	14.1	Engine power output (hp)	282
Length (m)	7.2	Number of forward gears	6
Width (m)	2.7	Number of reverse gears	2
Height (m)	2.92	Main weapon calibre (mm)	90
Max. road speed (km/h)	105	Auxiliary gun calibre (mm) x3	7.62
Fuel capacity (ℓ)	480	Ammunition for main weapon	50
Max. road range (km)	1,000	Ammunition for the auxiliary gun	6,000

Ratel 81 Mk3 specifications

Crew	2+3	Gradient (%)	60
Combat weight (t)	16.7	Trench (m)	1.15
Power-to-weight ratio (hp/t)	16.8	Engine power output (hp)	282
Length (m)	7.2	Number of forward gears	6
Width (m)	2.7	Number of reverse gears	2
Height (m)	2.5	Main weapon calibre (mm)	81
Max. road speed (km/h)	105	Auxiliary gun calibre (mm)	7.62
Fuel capacity (ℓ)	480	Ammunition for main weapon	148
Max. road range (km)	1,000	Ammunition for the auxiliary gun	1,200

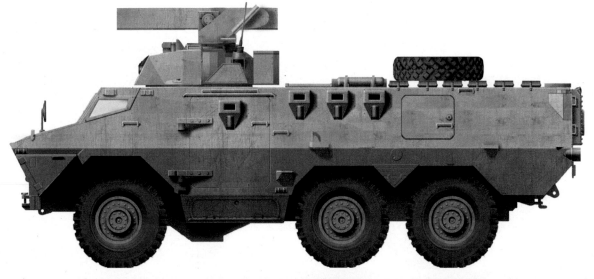

Ratel ZT-3A1 Mk3 specifications

Crew	4	Gradient (%)	60
Combat weight (t)	19.2	Trench (m)	1.15
Power-to-weight ratio (hp/t)	14.8	Engine power output (hp)	282
Length (m)	7.2	Number of forward gears	6
Width (m)	2.7	Number of reverse gears	2
Height (m)	3.34	Main weapon calibre (mm) x3	127
Max. road speed (km/h)	105	Auxiliary gun calibre (mm)	7.62
Fuel capacity (ℓ)	480	Ammunition for main weapon	12
Max. road range (km)	1,000	Ammunition for the auxiliary gun	1,200

Casspir Mk3 specifications

Crew	2+12	Gradient (%)	50
Combat weight (t)	10.7	Trench (m)	1
Power-to-weight ratio (hp/t)	15.5	Engine power output (hp)	166
Length (m)	6.9	Number of forward gears	6
Width (m)	2.5	Number of reverse gears	1
Height (m)	3.1	Main weapon calibre (mm)	7.62
Max. road speed (km/h)	90	Auxiliary gun calibre (mm)	-
Fuel capacity (ℓ)	200	Ammunition for main weapon	3,800
Max. road range (km)	800	Ammunition for the auxiliary gun	-

G6-45 specifications

Crew	6	Gradient (%)	40
Combat weight (t)	46	Trench (m)	1
Power-to-weight ratio (hp/t)	11.9	Engine power output (hp)	550
Length (m)	9.2	Number of forward gears	6
Width (m)	3.5	Number of reverse gears	1
Height (m)	3.4	Main weapon calibre (mm)	155
Max. road speed (km/h)	85	Auxiliary gun calibre (mm)	7.62
Fuel capacity (ℓ)	700	Ammunition for main weapon	39
Max. road range (km)	700	Ammunition for the auxiliary gun	2,000

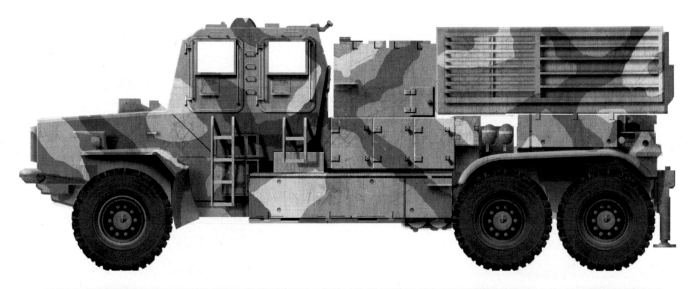

Bateleur FV2 specifications

Crew	5	Gradient (%)	70
Combat weight (t)	21.5	Trench (m)	0.5
Power-to-weight ratio (hp/t)	12.5	Engine power output (hp)	268
Length (m)	8.53	Number of forward gears	8
Width (m)	2.45	Number of reverse gears	1
Height (m)	3.12	Main weapon calibre (mm)	127
Max. road speed (km/h)	90	Auxiliary gun calibre (mm)	7.62
Fuel capacity (ℓ)	400	Ammunition for main weapon	40
Max. road range (km)	1,000	Ammunition for the auxiliary gun	1,000

Olifant Mk1A specifications

Crew	4	Gradient (%)	58
Combat weight (t)	56	Trench (m)	3.45
Power-to-weight ratio (hp/t)	13.39	Engine power output (hp)	750
Length (m)	7.56	Number of forward gears	2
Width (m)	3.39	Number of reverse gears	1
Height (m)	2.94	Main weapon calibre (mm)	105
Max. road speed (km/h)	45	Auxiliary gun calibre (mm)	7.62
Fuel capacity (ℓ)	1,240	Ammunition for main weapon	72
Max. road range (km)	350	Ammunition for the auxiliary gun	5,600

Olifant Mk1B specifications

Crew	4	Gradient (%)	51
Combat weight (t)	59	Trench (m)	3.45
Power-to-weight ratio (hp/t)	16.1	Engine power output (hp)	950
Length (m)	8.30	Number of forward gears	4
Width (m)	3.43	Number of reverse gears	2
Height (m)	3.04	Main weapon calibre (mm)	105
Max. road speed (km/h)	58	Auxiliary gun calibre (mm)	7.62
Fuel capacity (ℓ)	1,382	Ammunition for main weapon	65
Max. road range (km)	360	Ammunition for the auxiliary gun	6,000

Olifant Mk2 specifications

Crew	4	Gradient (%)	51
Combat weight (t)	60.5	Trench (m)	3.5
Power-to-weight ratio (hp/t)	17.35	Engine power output (hp)	1050
Length (m)	8.30	Number of forward gears	4
Width (m)	3.43	Number of reverse gears	2
Height (m)	3.04	Main weapon calibre (mm)	105
Max. road speed (km/h)	58	Auxiliary gun calibre (mm)	7.62
Fuel capacity (ℓ)	1,285	Ammunition for main weapon	64
Max. road range (km)	360	Ammunition for the auxiliary gun	6,600

TTD specifications

Crew	4	Gradient (%)	60
Combat weight (t)	58.3	Trench (m)	3.5
Power-to-weight ratio (hp/t)	21.16	Engine power output (hp)	1234
Length (m)	7.78	Number of forward gears	4
Width (m)	3.62	Number of reverse gears	2
Height (m)	2.99	Main weapon calibre (mm)	105
Max. road speed (km/h)	71	Auxiliary gun calibre (mm)	7.62
Fuel capacity (ℓ)	1,600	Ammunition for main weapon	54
Max. road range (km)	400	Ammunition for the auxiliary gun	2,000

Rooikat 76 Mk1D specifications

Crew	4	Gradient (%)	70
Combat weight (t)	28	Trench (m)	2
Power-to-weight ratio (hp/t)	20.1	Engine power output (hp)	563
Length (m)	7.1	Number of forward gears	6
Width (m)	2.9	Number of reverse gears	1
Height (m)	2.9	Main weapon calibre (mm)	76
Max. road speed (km/h)	120	Auxiliary gun calibre (mm)	7.62
Fuel capacity (ℓ)	540	Ammunition for main weapon	49
Max. road range (km)	1,000	Ammunition for the auxiliary gun	3,800

Rooikat 105 specifications

Crew	4	Gradient (%)	70
Combat weight (t)	28.5	Trench (m)	2
Power-to-weight ratio (hp/t)	20.1	Engine power output (hp)	563
Length (m)	7.1	Number of forward gears	6
Width (m)	2.9	Number of reverse gears	1
Height (m)	2.8	Main weapon calibre (mm)	105
Max. road speed (km/h)	120	Auxiliary gun calibre (mm)x2	7.62
Fuel capacity (ℓ)	540	Ammunition for main weapon	32
Max. road range (km)	1,000	Ammunition for the auxiliary gun	2,800

Rooikat ZA-35 SPAAG specifications

Crew	3	Gradient (%)	60
Combat weight (t)	32	Trench (m)	2
Power-to-weight ratio (hp/t)	20.1	Engine power output (hp)	563
Length (m)	7.3	Number of forward gears	6
Width (m)	2.9	Number of reverse gears	1
Height (m)	5	Main weapon calibre (mm) x2	35
Max. road speed (km/h)	120	Auxiliary gun calibre (mm)	-
Fuel capacity (ℓ)	540	Ammunition for main weapon	460
Max. road range (km)	1,000	Ammunition for the auxiliary gun	-

MAMBA Mk2 specifications

Crew	2+9	Gradient (%)	70
Combat weight (t)	6.8	Trench (m)	0.9
Power-to-weight ratio (hp/t)	18.1	Engine power output (hp)	123
Length (m)	5.39	Number of forward gears	8
Width (m)	2.21	Number of reverse gears	4
Height (m)	2.43	Main weapon calibre (mm) (see notes)	12.7
Max. road speed (km/h)	102	Auxiliary gun calibre (mm)	-
Fuel capacity (ℓ)	220	Ammunition for main weapon	1,000
Max. road range (km)	900	Ammunition for the auxiliary gun	-

MAMBA Mk3 specifications

Crew	2+9	Gradient (%)	70
Weight (t)	6.2	Trench (m)	0.9
Power-to-weight ratio (hp/t)	19.8	Engine power output (hp)	123
Length (m)	5.46	Number of forward gears	8
Width (m)	2.1	Number of reverse gears	4
Height (m)	2.5	Main weapon calibre (mm) (see notes)	12.7
Max. road speed (km/h)	102	Auxiliary gun calibre (mm)	-
Fuel capacity (ℓ)	160	Ammunition for main weapon	1,000
Max. road range (km)	800	Ammunition for the auxiliary gun	-

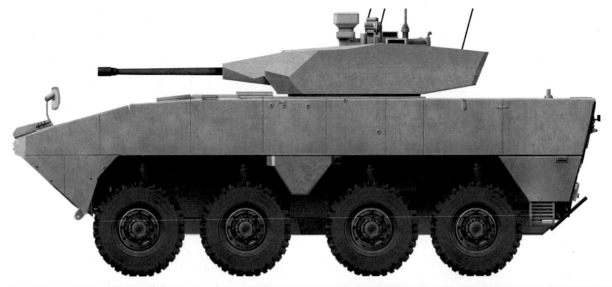

BADGER SECTION VARIANT specifications

Crew	4 + 7	Gradient (%)	60
Combat weight (t)	28	Trench (m)	2
Power-to-weight ratio (hp/t)	21.7	Engine power output (hp)	543
Length (m)	8.01	Number of forward gears	7
Width (m)	2.83	Number of reverse gears	1
Height (m)	3.44	Main weapon calibre (mm)	30
Max. road speed (km/h)	104	Auxiliary gun calibre (mm)	7.62
Fuel capacity (ℓ)	450	Ammunition for main weapon	400
Max. road range (km)	1,000	Ammunition for the auxiliary gun	4,000

BADGER MISSILE VARIANT specifications

Crew	4 + 7	Gradient (%)	60
Combat weight (t)	28	Trench (m)	2
Power-to-weight ratio (hp/t)	21.7	Engine power output (hp)	543
Length (m)	8.01	Number of forward gears	7
Width (m)	2.83	Number of reverse gears	1
Height (m)	3.44	Main weapon calibre (mm) x4	127
Max. road speed (km/h)	104	Auxiliary gun calibre (mm)	7.62
Fuel capacity (ℓ)	450	Ammunition for main weapon	12
Max. road range (km)	1,000	Ammunition for the auxiliary gun	4,000

A combined arms demonstration of various armoured vehicles including Olifant Mk1A, Rooikat 76 Mk1D, Ratel 20 Mk3 and Ratel 60 Mk3. A fire belt action (Vuurgordel) would see such a formation delivering rapid fire with main and secondary weapons for 20 seconds at possible or suspected enemy positions along the axis of advance. (R. Fouche)

A G6-45 Self-Propelled Howitzer-Vehicle with two Rooivalk Combat Support Helicopters overhead (R. Fouche)

A tank troop of Olifant Mk1A MBTs engaging a target during a public capability display with their GT3 105mm main gun. The GT3 is accurate to 50cm x 50cm (19.6in x 19.6in) at ranges up to 2km (1.24mi). (R. Fouche)

A Ratel Mk3 command vehicle armed with a 12.7mm machine gun as seen on a public display. Notable are the extra antennae for the additional communications equipment it carries. (R. Fouche)

Exceptional mobility, good armament, and balanced protection make the Rooikat 76 Mk1D one of the most formidable armoured cars in the world. Here the Rooikat is poised for a public Night Shoot at Muizenberg (Sunrise Beach) on 19 February 2019. (J.van Zyl)

The Olifant Mk2 is one of the most advanced MBTs in Southern Africa. Here it is showcasing its performance on the mobility course during AAD 2018. (D.Venter)

Two Casspir 106 Recoilless rifle weapons platforms are seen here, each armed with a 106mm M40 recoilless rifle which is located on a platform at the rear of the vehicle. The HEAT round is capable of penetrating 450mm (17.8in) RHA and can be accurately used at a range of 1.1km (0.68mi). (J.van Zyl)

Two Badger section variants during trials of its bush protection kit. Notable is its dual hull design consisting of an inner and outer hull, between which an add-on armour package can be fitted for additional protection against HEAT projectiles. (Denel Land Systems)

7
Olifant Mk1A Main Battle Tank

THE AFRICAN ELEPHANT

The Olifant Mk1A MBT takes its Afrikaans name from the African Elephant. The Olifant is the largest land animal, and thus, the Olifant MBT is aptly named as it is the heaviest military vehicle in the then SADF and post-democracy SANDF. The Olifant is popularly referred to as *Moemsie*, a cartoon elephant of the 1980s fame.

DEVELOPMENT

The Olifant Mk1A was the final evolutionary development of the British Centurions in South African service before the end of the Cold War. During 1953, South Africa, as part of the Commonwealth, purchased 87 Mk3 and 116 Mk5 Centurions from Great Britain. The first Centurian (R74783) was received the same year for training at the School of Armour. During the 1960s South Africa sought to purchase Mirage fighter aeroplanes from France and sold 100 Centurions to Switzerland to generate the required funds. As part of the purchase agreement, Switzerland was allowed to pick the best 100 Centurions from the South African inventory, which they did, virtually halving the South African tank capability. In the years that followed, the remaining tanks were used for training and large-scale exercises such as those held in 1966.

In 1964, the UN enacted a voluntary arms embargo on South Africa. Regardless of the sanctions, South Africa was able to obtain some of the equipment and parts necessary for the upkeep of the Centurion fleet with the exception of the 650hp (485kW) water-cooled V-12 Rolls Royce Meteor engine which was prone to overheating in the warm African weather. Furthermore, the strain brought on by the rocky terrain took its toll on the Centurions' road wheels and suspension. The changing global political environment against South Africa necessitated an increased requirement on self-reliance which led to the establishment of ARMSCOR in 1964, which would take on procurement, research and development tasks. With some sleight of hand and creative wording, ARMSCOR was able to procure diesel engines from General Motors under the pretext of them being used for farming. Although suitable,

the engines, meant for the cold weather use of Europe, regularly overheated in the African conditions. General Motors got wind of the engines' final destination and pulled the supply thereof in 1970.

In 1973, ARMSCOR acquired several air-cooled Continental V-12 petrol engines used in the M46/47 Patton which produced 810hp (604kW). With some creative modifications, they were installed in the South African Centurions. However, the new engines were far from perfect as they consumed a ridiculous amount of fuel, limiting the operational range off-road to just 40km. Additionally, the original tiller bars for driving were replaced by a steering handlebar system. Besides the two test models built by 61 Base Workshop, another six were produced by Sandock Austral, and all nine were pushed into service as an interim measure as the *Skokiaan* (an African alcoholic drink). At the same time, the Centurion Mk5A was being developed, nicknamed *Semel* (bran/cereal) which referred to its project development code name. Using the same engine as the Skokiaan, a total of 35 Semel were built from 1974 and featured the repositioning of the air filters (to avoid them getting clogged), increased fuel capacity (1400l), redesigned steering, and brakes which made use of hydraulics. Due to the increased threat of T-54/55 MBTs in Angola, the 35 Semel were sent to Walvis Bay (SWA) in 1976 to serve as a deterrent. Meanwhile, trials on the *Semel 2* variant continued at the School of Armour. Due to problems sourcing more engines, the Semel 2 project was cancelled.

While the interim Semel and Skokiaan were being produced the SAAC submitted a request to upgrade of the Centurion fleet to the standards of the Israeli *Sho't*. This request saw the birth of the Olifant MBT project which involved cooperation between SARSC, ARMSCOR and Barlow's through the subsidiary Barlow's Heavy Engineering, which established a division called the OMC in 1976. Lacking sufficient Centurion hulls due to the sale of a hundred Centurions in the 1960s an extensive search led to the acquisition of 200 Mk5 and Mk7 Centurion tanks in various states of disrepair from Jordan and India.

Olifant Mk1A – public display. (R. Fouche)

Skokiaan – School of Armour. (D.Venter)

Olifant Mk1A – In the foreground with a Olifant Mk2 in the background. De Brug. (J. van Zyl)

Olifant Mk1A – De Brug. (F. Esterhuizen)

1976, followed by a second in 1977, and a third in 1978.

The Olifant Mk1 was officially introduced in 1978 and featured a 750hp (559kW) diesel engine coupled to a semi-automatic transmission. Production commenced in 1978 and lasted until 1984 making use of the Mk5 and Mk7 Centurions available. As luck would have it, South Africa confiscated a shipment of T-55 tanks bound for Tanzania from a cargo ship which docked in Durban harbour and subsequent trials against these T-55s revealed several inadequacies of the Olifant Mk1. Luckily, development of the Olifant Mk1A had already begun in 1981, with production starting in 1983. The new Olifant Mk1A upgrade of the Olifant Mk1 was ready for service from 1985 onward and featured a stabilised and locally produced 105mm GT3-52 calibre semi-automatic quick-firing gun. The FCS was improved and a passive night vision sight on a night elbow installed as well as a laser rangefinder. A recognisable difference between the Olifant Mk1 and Olifant Mk1A is that the spare tracks were moved from the front glacis to either side of the forward hull, above the fender flaps. Several Olifant Mk1As are used for training purposes by the SANDF while the remainder are in preservation storage.

DESIGN FEATURES

The Olifant is a prime example of what ingenuity and technical expertise can accomplish. It took a long time and much effort, but by the time we had finished, almost nothing (30%) of the old Centurions remained except the characteristic hulls, turret shells and track skirts.

Major General (retd) Roland de Vries

Significant changes made to create the Olifant include the engine, main gun (84mm to 105mm), diesel fuel tanks, driver's control systems, ammunition storage, commander's copula, upgraded gun control, sights, air cleaners, communication systems, rotary junction box, explosion suppression system, engine exhaust smoke generator and turret cooling fan. Additional storage bins were added to the exterior rear of the turret and spare tracks were kept on the frontal glacis plate of the hull. The first PPM of the Olifant Mk1 was sent to the SA Army School of Armour at Tempe military base for testing in

Mobility

The Olifant Mk1A has 508mm (20in) of ground clearance and can ford 1.2m (3.9ft) of water without preparation. The Olifant Mk1A retained the Horstman suspension from the Centurion. A new rail system was installed allowing the power pack to be quickly changed in the field with the use of a crane in less than 30 minutes. The South African environment produced an exceptional amount of fine dust which necessitated the fitting of improved air filters which allowed the optimum use of the new Continental 29l turbo-charged air-cooled V12 diesel engine which produced 750hp (13.39hp/t). The engine was coupled to a new improved and robust semi-automatic Allison transmission system with two forward (low and high range) and one reverse gear allowing the Olifant Mk1A to achieve 45km/h (28mph) on roads, which was a significant improvement over the Centurion Mk5's 35km/h (22mph), and allowed acceleration from 0-30km/h (0-19mph) in 15 seconds on a flat surface. Steering is done via a handlebar system. The added improvements added 5t of additional mass, though this is negligible considering the level of improvements made to the overall engine.

Olifant Mk1A – Live fire exercise. (SA Army Armour Formation)

Endurance and logistics

The fuel capacity was improved from 458ℓ (121gal) of the Centurion Mk5 to 1,240ℓ (328gal) in the Olifant Mk1A. Subsequently, the Olifant Mk1A could travel 350km (217mi) on-road, 240km

Olifant Mk1 ARV – Exercise Thunder Chariot, Army Battle School. (SA Army Armour Formation)

(149mi) off-road, and 150km (93mi) on sand as opposed to the Centurion Mk5's 190km (118mi) on road, 80km (49mi) off-road, and 50km (31mi) on sand. Considerable effort was made into making the Olifant Mk1A easier to maintain by ensuring that both mechanical and electronic subsystems were easy to access as the tank was to be employed on more extended missions over rugged and variable terrain with less logistical support than before. The Olifant Mk1A's tracks consisted of 108 links over twenty-four road wheels (12 per side), each of which had an average service life of 300-500km (186-311mi) which necessitated regular maintenance and replacement. Operations in Angola proved the merit of the upgrades which reduced crew fatigue considerably.

The Olifant Mk1A is equipped with two 7.62mm BMG, one in the coaxial position and one at the commander's cupola. At least 5,600 7.62mm rounds consisting of 28 belts of 200 rounds each are carried.

The Olifant Mk1A features tactical radio communication which allowed for reliable command and control. This proved very useful in the thick Angolan bush, enhancing the tank's force multiplier effect on the battlefield. Extra whip aerials for the radio were carried in a tube on the hull as they had a tendency to bend when doing

bundu bashing. Each Olifant Mk1A carried its own water in jerry cans, and a cooking stove, tool kit, tow bar, cable and spare parts in the tote. The Olifant Mk1A relied on daily replenishment from the administration and logistic support vehicles of the echelon.

Vehicle layout

The Olifant Mk1A carries a standard crew complement of four consisting of the commander, gunner, loader and driver. The commander's station is located on the right side of the turret and retained the commander's cupola of the Centurion, which offered a 360-degree field of vision through eight vision blocks. An additional vision block is provided, which can swivel independently. Entry and exit from this station is achieved through a hatch. Also on the right side of the turret, just in front and below the commander's station is the gunner's station. On the left of the turret is the loader's station. Entry and exit for the commander and gunner are through the commander's hatch while the loader has a separate hatch. The driver's compartment is located at the front and right of the hull, from where he has 90-degree forward vision through two driver's episcopes. The driver can enter and exit the vehicle through a hatch located above his seat.

Olifant Mk1A – Equipped with mine rollers. (SA Army Armour Formation)

Main armament

The Olifant Mk1A was initially equipped with a 105mm L7 rifled gun barrel sourced from Israel. An improved South African produced 105mm GT3 52 calibre semi-automatic quick-firing gun manufactured by LEW was later fitted.

The GT3 105mm initially made use of the L52A3 APDS, M456 HEAT and M156 HESH rounds sourced from Israel. The L52A3 has a velocity of 1,326m/s (4,350 ft/s) and can penetrate 300mm (11.8in) of RHA at zero degrees. The M456 HEAT round travel velocity is 1,000m/s (3,281 f/s) and can effectively penetrate 420mm (16.5in) of RHA at zero degrees. The M156 HESH velocity is 731m/s (2,398 f/s) can penetrate 310mm (12.2in) of RHA at zero degrees.

The Israeli M111 was acquired by South Africa in the mid-80s as the principle APFSDS-T round used by the Olifant Mk1A. It has a muzzle velocity of 1,455m/s (4,773 ft/s) and can penetrate 390mm (15.4in) of RHA. The Israelis successfully tested the round on a T-72A MBT, penetrating its frontal glacis, however, it was not able to penetrate the frontal turret. The M111 caused such consternation for the Russians that they hurriedly redesigned the T-72A frontal glacis. Needless to say, the SADF use of the M111 in Angola against T-55 and T-62 tanks was a spectacular success. The round is commonly referred to as the Fin Mk1 in South Africa.

During the mid-90s South Africa acquired the 2nd generation APFSDS-T round known as the, M429 or locally as the M2A1 Mk2 (Fin Mk2 Improved). The muzzle velocity is 1,450m/s (4,757 ft/s) and can penetrate 420mm (16.5in) of RHA at zero degrees.

In 2011 the Olifant family received the Rheinmetall Denel Munitions 3rd generation 105mm APFSDS-T round known as the M426 or Fin Mk3. It can penetrate 450mm (17.7in) of RHA at zero degrees, has a velocity of 1,450m/s (4,757 ft/s), a combat range of 2km (1.24mi) and is accurate to 50cm x 50 cm (19.6in x 19.6in).

The Olifant Mk1A can fire the Denel M9210 HE round which contains a TNT/HNS filling and an effective blast radius of 17m (56ft). The round is fired with a muzzle velocity of 700m/s (2,296 ft/s) to a maximum range of 9km (5.6mi). M416 white phosphorus rounds which are used to create a smoke screen can also be fired at a distance of 9km (5.6mi) and travels at 730m/s (2,395 ft/s).

A new electrical gun and turret drive was developed for the Olifant Mk1A, while improved gun stabilisation was also incorporated. The turret drive can traverse the turret 360 degrees in 30 seconds.

The fighting compartment saw improvements to the layout of the 105mm ammunition, which increased the total carrying capacity to 72 rounds, significantly more than the Centurion Mk13 which carries 64 rounds.

Fire control system

The FCS was also improved, which allowed quicker and more accurate engagements. The original Centurion x6 magnification stadia sight was replaced with the Eloptro MSZ-2 two-channel day and night sight. The right-hand sight channel provided x8 magnification for daytime and the left x7.2 magnification via an image-intensifier night elbow. Co-mounted was a laser range finder which was accurate to 10km. Data from the rangefinder was by design fed into the split range drum, which applied elevation to the main gun. Tests revealed that the system is accurate within 50cm x 50 cm (19.6in x 19.6in) at 2km (1.24mi) which was perfect for the South African "*Louveld*" (open stretches of grass plains) but would prove overcomplicated for the average 100m (109yd) engagements in the Angolan bush.

Protection

The Olifant Mk1A retained the Centurion armour which consisted of 76mm (2.99in) on the frontal glacis at 58 degrees, 152mm frontal turret (6in), 51mm (2in) on the sides, 40mm (1.57in) on top and 29mm (1.14in) in the rear of the tank. The armoured side skirts which are 4.5mm (0.17in) thick were manufactured from armoured steel in South Africa and serve to detonate HEAT rounds before they reached the hull. Even though the Olifant Mk1A can penetrate a T-54/55 and T-62 frontally at 2km, the former armed with a 100mm gun and latter armed with a 115mm main gun can also destroy the Olifant Mk1A. The Olifant Mk1A is also vulnerable to RPG-7.

One bank of four 81mm smoke grenade launchers is located either side of the turret, replacing the old smoke grenade launchers of the Centurion Mk5 and Mk7. Recent improvements also include the fitting of a protective frame to protect against vegetation while bundu bashing.

Olifant Mk1A – Bore sighting before departing on Ops Hooper. (C. van Schoor)

THE OLIFANT FAMILY

ARV

At least one ARV based on the hull of the Olifant Mk1 was completed by OMC in 1979, with an additional two being ready in 1984 for use in exercise Thunder Chariot. The Olifant ARV's primary task is to extract disabled vehicles under enemy fire. At the rear is a spade ground anchor which enables the main winch equipped with a 58kw (78hp) motor to pull a 120t load via a 3:1 snatch block. On the rear-right is an excavator digging arm. The ARV has a crew of four who

Olifant Mk1A – Attack on 59 Brigade as viewed through the commander's cupola. (C. van Schoor)

have at their disposal jacks, cables, chains, power saws, spades and an oxyacetylene cutting and welding torch which is stored in the exterior side bins, and is equipped with a small crane jib at the rear which is used to tow a damaged vehicle out of action. One would be assigned per tank squadron and four per tank regiment. The ARVs were assigned to 61 Mech. A total of 14 ARV's were built.

Mine clearing rollers and plough kit

SADF/SANDF evaluated the use of mine-clearing roller and plough kit for the Olifant Mk1A. Southern African conditions proved that a plough-type, electro-hydraulic dozer blade was not feasible as test models bent in the hard soil and could not uproot trees. Additionally, the extra strain on the MBT would overheat the engine, especially on sandy terrain.

THE CONTRIBUTIONS OF SOUTH AFRICAN ARMOUR TO THE OPERATIONS OF 1987/88 MODULER, HOOPER, PACKER, EXCITE AND HILTI

Brigadier General (retd) André Retief, who was a Major at the time commanding the tank echelon, provides an overview of the use of armour during 1987/88.

Armour's contribution

Armour contributed the following towards the operations:

- Armoured Car (Eland 90) Squadron to Sector 10 Oskati
- Armoured Car/Anti-Tank (Ratel 90) Squadron to 32 Battalion (the only one to include the ZT3 Missile AT Systems)
- Armoured Car (Ratel 90) Squadron to 61 Mech
- Armoured Car (Ratel 90) Squadron to 4 SAI
- Tank (Olifant) Squadron to 4 SAI
- Tank (Olifant) Squadron to 61 Mech

Planning

The above forces, including their Armour components, were committed in piecemeal fashion, often "too little too late", as the operations escalated. This gradual escalation can be attributed to changing threat perceptions of the opposing forces, changing political objectives, changing strategic and operational objectives, and typical "mission creep".

Implementation

At the start of these operations, the only armour involved in the conflict were the AC squadrons deployed to Sector 10, 32 Battalion and 61 Mech, all stationed internally in Namibia. This was followed by 32 Battalion deployed into Angola with their armour element (the only one with Ratel ZT3s). Later 61 Mech with their AC squadron deployed into Angola. Then 4 SAI with ACs and Olifant squadron

T-55 – A 59 Brigade tank destroyed in its defensive position by an Olifant Mk1A. (C. van Schoor)

when an enemy target was hit compared to the APFSDS rounds. The HEAT rounds also did not feature a SAD which would arm after penetrating 150 mm. Due to the thick bush which limited vision, armoured engagements were seldom further than 150m and often as close as 50m. The use of HEAT rounds allowed the Olifant to instantly engage dug-in T-54/55s located behind defensive sand walls to be quickly followed by another HEAT or APFSDS round.

As part of Operation Moduler, E-squadron engaged FAPLA's 16th Brigade during the battle of Chambinga on the 9th of November 1987. Lt. Hein Fourie destroyed the first enemy T-54/55 with an Olifant Mk1A, followed by another to the gun of Lt. Abrie Strauss and his crew.

Operation Hooper was launched on 2 January 1988 and saw F-Squadron School of Armour, under Major Tim Rudman, take the lead to dislodge FAPLA's 21st Brigade from the River Cuatir through a midnight bombardment from across the river. On 13 January F-Squadron led an attack on 21st FAPLA Brigade as part of Combat Group Charlie and successfully took the objective.

Later during the offensive on Tumpo 1 and Tumpo 2, a counterattack by Cuban forces soon followed in which one Olifant Mk1A was damaged, two Olifant Mk1 from the Citizen Force Squadron Mooi River were detracked by anti-tank mines while a third threw its tracks. Despite repeated attempts to salvage the tanks, they had to be abandoned due to intense enemy artillery and ground fire. The two detracked Olifant tanks can still be found where they were immobilized while the third was captured intact by FAPLA. The turret was shipped to the Soviet Union while the hull can be found at Menongue airport in Angola. Additionally, a Ratel was destroyed and four SADF soldiers killed while the Cuban forces and FAPLA lost 21 T-54/55s and suffered 480 casualties.

Corporal (retd) W. Surmon, Olifant Mk1A Gunner

followed by 61 Mechanised Battalion Group who also received an Olifant MBT squadron.

During Operation Hooper and Packer a tank regiment was used with infantry support, albeit with only two squadrons. Eventually, by the time of Operation Packer and Excite there was a Tank Regiment (minus one squadron). Initially, all the armour elements were used in the infantry support role and employed integrated with their respective battalions.

OLIFANT IN ACTION

The South African Border War came to a finale in Sector 20 during Operations Moduler, Hooper and Packer and in Sector 10 during Operation Excite. Two squadrons of Olifant Mk1 (Citizen Force Squadron) and Mk1A (National Servicemen Squadron), Comprising of 3 Troops of 3 Tanks (51, 51A, 51B); (52, 52A, 52B); (53, 53A, 53B) Command Tank (50) 2nd in Command (50A) and Spare Tank (59S – Fitted with Mine Rollers) each, giving a combined total of 24 tanks for Operation Modular, Hooper and Packer and later in June 1988, 13 Tanks were deployed for Ops Excite. The tanks were sent to Angola to stop the Cuban and FAPLA advances to Jamba (Sector 20) and SWAVEK (Sector 10). In sector 20, they would face off against 70 T-54/55s MBTs, and over 105 T54/55s in Sector 10. The Olifant tanks and Ratel 90s would engage FAPLA tanks and armoured cars.

The SADF jumped to the aid of their allies, UNITA who were facing annihilation. The Cuban and Soviet-backed FAPLA gathered eight brigades and an extensive auxiliary support force (aided by Soviet advisors) and advanced east-south-east from Cuito Cuanavale to attack UNITA's primary operating bases at Mavinga and Jamba. What followed was the largest conventional battle on African soil, since World War 2. 61 Mechanized Battalion Group broke 47 Brigade at the Lomba River.

The Olifant Mk1A made its combat debut with E-Squadron during Ops Moduler in late 1987, and on 3 Jan 1988 during Operation Hooper. The SADF tank crews preferred using HEAT rounds which were equally effective against soft-skinned and armoured vehicles. Even though the thick bush can prematurely detonate a HEAT round, it produced a much more visible impact

CONCLUSION

The Olifant Mk1A became a true African MBT as it had to be adapted to suit the unique operational and tactical requirements found in the Southern African battlespace. With some creativity and ingenuity, the South African arms industry was able to upgrade a 40-year-old MBT into one that went toe to toe against an enemy with numerically superior tanks. The Olifant Mk1A was soon to have a facelift in the form of the Mk1B, but unlike before, the Mk1B would be a complete rebuild which can face down and beat the potent T-72M.

A soldier's account – The Olifant Mk1A training

I can remember back in 1983 we arrived at the School of Armour, 1 SSB, Bloemfontein. We attended lectures where the instructors

T-55 – A 59 Brigade tank destroyed in its defensive position by an Olifant Mk1A. (C. van Schoor)

would give us information one had to learn about the Olifant. Our knowledge was tested on paper and after that in practice. As a driver, I was very interested in its fuel consumption. Bear in mind the Olifant weighed 56t, and the distance one could travel on a full tank of diesel in the bush was 250km (155mi). The top speed was about 45kph (28mph) on a gravel road.

A successful tank crew has to work as a team, take instructions from the commander and to listen to what the gunner has to say regarding the targets that have been lined up and of course not to forget the loader as he needs to concentrate on what round needs to be put in the breach ridge before the gunner shoots the round off may it be HE, AP or smoke.

I'll never forget the first time I climbed into the driver's compartment and took a seat [with] my head out of the hatch. To turn the tank left or right there was a handle with two grips on it that look like the bicycle handle crossbar. A massive brake pedal where you could put both feet onto the brakes for emergency stopping with the accelerator next to it. The gear lever was on the right-hand side where you could select your gears from low to high. When driving your tank in low gear one had to watch your rev indicator till it goes to red, take your foot off the accelerator change the gear to high and then push the accelerator down to get maximum speed.

What I can also remember where all the instruments that were on the right. You had your start button, your switch off button plus your fuel tanks. There were two fuel tank gauges, and there was [a] gun indicator showing exactly which position was the gun maybe 12:00 or 6:00 you always know where it is especially when your hatches are closed.

I remember driving the Olifant for the first time, and it was an adrenaline rush. We went to De Brug just west of Bloemfontein where there was an extensive obstacle course which I can remember climbing a very steep gradient till we got to the top. Then the tank would crash down on the other side of this very steep hill, and with speed, one had to put on brakes as there was a big pool of water waiting for you and if you went too fast that water would go into the driver's hatch, leaving the driver completely wet. Drivers were issued a pair of goggles to keep any dust out of our eyes and a scarf around my mouth so that I could breathe as if there was too much fine dust while travelling on sandy roads.

At the shooting range in Lohatla, I had to maintain a speed of 14km an hour as the gunner would line up his targets. Driving while the gunner was shooting was exhilarating as you had to concentrate on where you were driving. Luckily the gun stabilization system allowed the gunner always to get hits on target.

I can remember when the crew commander would say "TARGET 11", immediately the gunner followed the crew commander orders, lined up his target with the instructions and the gunner would say "target on". The crew commander would say "fire", and the gunner would say "firing now" and there was a massive boom.

Looking through the periscopes as the gun fired you would see the flash of the actual gun and then all of a sudden a massive dust cloud that obscured your vision. Once the dust had cleared, you would see the explosion of the round hitting the target, which was very impressive.

Listening on the radio to the crew commander shouting to the loader to load the next round, have the gunner lined up his next target and of course telling me the direction where to drive to.

I must say the excitement that goes through the actual tank while you're driving and with all the crew working at the same time is an experience that one never forgets.

Another highlight of being a driver was after having all the fun on the actual shooting range you had to drive back to the hangar and park your tank, switch off then, clean the compartment and make ready for the next day.

To make preparations for the next day one had to take the side panels off as you had a lot of tools with you being a driver and you need to take these heavy plates off and start greasing all the grease nipples on the bogie wheels.

It was amazing to see how many grease nipples there were on an Olifant, and it took some time to grease them all. An additional function of a tank driver was to help load the rounds through a porthole on the side of the tank, and there's a picture of me doing that job.

To start the tank in the morning was very exciting as the engine roared to life. Driving a tank was an experience I'll never forget.

Corporal (retd) M. Hume Olifant Mk1A Driver

Olifant Mk1A – Gunnery training Lohatla shooting range. (M. Hume)

A soldier's account – Olifant Mk1A MBT at Tumpo

Having been involved in some severe tank battles, I have had a lot of interest in checking up on the books written, and history of the conflict in Angola specifically in Operation Hooper in which we were involved. Nowhere can I find a reference to our regiment, only 61 Mech tanks. So this short story is dedicated to the men of Regiment Molopo and to Corporal Leon van Wyk who lost his life, on the 25 February 1988 during [the] Tumpu 2 attack.

I was a young Captain in Regiment Molopo, trained as a squadron commander in armour. Regiment Molopo had been an armoured car regiment using Eland 90 and Eland 60. During the last two years, we had converted to a tank regiment, at the School of Armour, and done extensive training at Army Battle School Lohatla. We were freshly trained and very eager. We were on 24 hours standby when the telegram arrived, and it was a blur of travelling, medical examinations, kitting up, flights travelling into Angola and then in SAMIL 50 and 100 ground transports to the front.

We took over a squadron of tanks from Regiment Pretoria, whose members looked like props from a Mad Max movie. The Olifant bins were broken, side armour plates covering the tracks were missing, but they were all battle-ready and reliable.

Our first Operation, 14 February 1988, we had been allocated to 61 Mechanised Battalion Group under the command of Mike Muller. We were to be the reserve force for the main attack, as well as be prepared to cut off any enemy reinforcements. We had travelled all day to get to our position when we approached a large "*shona*" (open area), about 2km wide. We stopped in the bush line just before the "*shona*", and were observing when suddenly on the opposite bush line a T-55 drove out. It must have seen us because he did a mad dash, u-turn, bellowing black diesel smoke back into the bush. At the same time, we were given orders to do a firing barrage and then charge over the "*shona*".

My bravo tank (named Oddball), had observed the T-55 and aimed at the spot it had entered the bush and fired an ADPFS round. Crew commander Sgt

Olifant Mk1A – Call sign T11 from Regiment Molopo engaging enemy T-55 tank during twilight. (D. Kuhnert)

Olifant Mk1A – Destroyed enemy T-55 cooking off. (D. Kuhnert)

a barrel of a gun. Directly in front of him was a T-55. Scotty sank down into the Olifant and shouted "TANK!", and at the same time, the enemy tank fired at them. The enemy tank was about 100m (109 yd) away, and their round fell short into the ground just off their right track. The crew were doing automatic reaction and before they could fire back a second round was fired at them! We later discussed this and came to a conclusion; it had an automatic loader, which would indicate that it was not T-55. Amazingly they had not made a correction and the second shot missed again. Scotty's crew pumped an APDFS round through the tank, and there was a double explosion. A BRDM was directly behind the enemy tanks and suffered the same fate. Two kills with one shot. Scotty had a stutter after this incident.

Scotty got the first kill with his ADPFS round, which had gone straight through the engine.

After we charged across the "*shona*" in line abreast, we were given the instruction to do a 90-degree swing to the right and continue at walking speed. This allowed the supportes (UNITA infantry) to climb off the Olifant and walk between our tanks, doing cleaning up. We had not moved 100m (109 yd) when I suddenly saw a tank dug in facing out into the "*shona*", on my right side. I immediately swung the turret onto the target while simultaneously giving firing commands. My gunner Anton was screaming that he can't see anything! The tank was too close, and the x7 magnification sight was blurred. I held the barrel on target and told Anton to fire with the T-55 only 30m away. I swear it sounded like a church bell when we shot it. It seemed like flames were peeling back onto us. I saw a crew member, running, scrabbling, on all fours trying to get away, and in the heat of the moment, I overrode and steered the barrel onto him. The crew in the meantime had followed standard procedure, reloaded, and I fired the second round. That was the end of him, he just about evaporated.

My Alpha tank took out the next T-55 to my right. The enemy crew commander climbed out, and stood on the hull with his pants on his knees and his hands on his hips looking very arrogant, but most probably in a total shock and confusion when the next round went between his legs. We took two more kills.

After moving another 600m (656yd), I contacted the squadron commander (T10) and asked if they were still with us. By this time it was total chaos on the radios, and explosions all around us. I made out that the main force was some way behind us at a standstill. I radioed Scotty and asked him to fire a green flare to show our position. Scotty bent down in the turret to grab a flare behind him, when he looked up and forward he was looking down

I stopped our progress to regroup and get our bearings. We kept a vigilant watch, and after a few minutes our supportes' leader came to my tank and asked me to follow him. We had been given basic training in Portuguese to communicate with our UNITA allies, so when he asked me for *medico*, I thought he was asking for a medic, as he was pointing towards a group of FAPLA soldiers lying on the ground, mostly wounded. I replied no medico, as we had no medic with us. He gave a command to the guards, and they promptly emptied their magazines into them. Talk about miscommunication.

It was becoming twilight, and I was about to give the order to turn about and join the main force when suddenly I saw a brown tank come speeding from my left to right approximately 200m (218yd) in front of us and doing about 55kph (34mph). I shouted, tank 200m (218yd) and I swing barrel to the left. ON ANTON ON, FIRE, FIRING NOW. The round hit the centre of the turret. The tank comes to a stop, and we fired a second APDFS round which hit the enemy tanks ammunition which started to explode. A massive *VVVOOO*, and an orange flame shot 30m into the air which silhouette the entire time we move back to the main force. At least our forces could see us from where we were coming from.

Up until today, I am convinced that two of the seven tanks we took were T-62s. Something always troubled me about the silhouette of that last tank and the way the barrel drooped in conjunction with the quick-fire rate of the tank which fired at my Bravo tank. Maybe one day I'll find out.

Major (retd) D. Kuhnert Olifant Mk1A Commander

8

Olifant Mk1B Main Battle Tank

THE AFRICAN ELEPHANT

The Olifant Mk1B is a rebuild of the Olifant Mk1A adapted for the African battlespace and based on the lessons learned from the South African Border War. This design only kept the turret mantlet, drive ring and hull sides, bottom plates and ring gear.

DEVELOPMENT

Unlike the Mk1A, which is an upgrade from the Centurion Mk5 and Mk7 hull, the Mk1B was a complete rebuild and in doing so left behind the legacy, features and outer look of the Centurion MBT. Development of the Mk1B commenced soon after the Mk1 went into production in 1981. OMC set out to design and build an interim MBT that would improve on the shortcomings of the Mk1A which were exposed during the South African Border War such as inadequate armour, poor mobility, improved firepower and taxing maintenance requirements. The Mk1B was designed to face off against T-54/55, T-62, and T-72M MBTs, which are equipped respectively with 100mm, 115mm and 125mm main guns. The primary focus, therefore, was placed on protection followed by improved firepower capabilities, then mobility, and lastly reduction of vehicle maintenance and crew fatigue. Trials were held at DeBrug, Lohatla and Vastrap in 1986 for five months with two complete Olifant crews and an additional driver in tail.

A total of 44 Mk1B would be built in two batches of 22 each starting in 1991. South Africa is the sole user of the Mk1B of which 26 were upgraded to Mk2 standard in 2005. Presently the remaining Mk1Bs are in environmentally controlled warehouse storage at Wallmansthal.

DESIGN FEATURES

The design, development and production of the Mk1B were undertaken due to the increasing number of Soviet-supplied tanks in Southern Africa. It was particularly feared that the Soviet-backed Cuban forces in Angola would ship T-72M MBTs to the Angolan theatre. The possible deployment of T-72M MBTs necessitated a much better protected, mobile and more lethal South African MBT than the Mk1A.

Mobility

Although the African battlespace favours a wheeled configuration, the Mk1B was envisaged to retain its predecessor's role as an MBT. The Mk1B can ford 1.2m (3.9ft) of water without preparation. With regards to the mobility question, the Mk1B kept the Continental 291 turbo-charged V12 diesel engine of the Mk1A. Improvements to the engine enabled an additional 200hp (139kW) which totalled 950hp (708kW) and raised the horsepower per tonne from 13.39hp/t to 16.1hp/t; a necessary improvement considering that the Mk1B weighed 3t more than the Mk1A. A new automatic transmission called AMTRA 3 was assembled by Gear Ratio and installed in the Mk1B which provided double-differential steering (four forward gears and two reverse), two-speed mechanical steering drive and hydraulic retarder. The additional 200hp (139kW) and new automatic transmission allowed the Mk1B to accelerate from 0-30km/h (0-19mph) in 11.5 seconds on flat terrain and achieve a top speed of 58km/h (36mph) on road which was a further improvement over the Mk1A's 45km/h (28mph).

The old Centurion Horstmann suspension was replaced with a new torsion bar suspension system with hydraulic dampers which provides an overall 300-400% improvement in wheel travel compared to the Mk1A. Bump stops were fitted to all the road wheels in order to improve off-road mobility while telescopic dampers were fitted to the front and two back stations to reduce rocking when stopping the tank. Steering is done via a yoke instead of tillers. The overall result of the improvements is a less taxing driving experience for driver and crew, especially over rough terrain.

Olifant Mk1B – SA Armour Museum. (D. Venter)

Endurance and logistics

The fuel capacity was increased from 1,240ℓ (328gal) in the Mk1A, to 1,382ℓ (365gal) in the Mk1B. The MBT can travel 360km (224mi) on road, 240km (149mi) off-road and 150km (93mi) on sand. With the redesigning of the hull, the engine compartment was extended, allowing more space for easier maintenance and if required, removal and replacement of the entire power pack. To reduce the frequency of road wheel replacements an outer polyurethane surface was applied which increased the road wheel life from 300km (186mi) of the Mk1A to 1,200km (745mi) on the Mk1B. With the extended engine compartment which lengthened the overall hull, an additional track link was added which brought the total to 109 track links on each side.

Olifant Mk1B – Front view. SA Armour Museum. (D. Venter)

The Mk1B is equipped with one 7.62mm coaxial machine gun with a 2,000 round ready bin that replaced the 200 round boxes used in the Mk1A. At least 6,000 rounds of 7.62mm are carried. The Mk1B features

Olifant Mk1B – Side view. SA Armour Museum. (D. Venter)

tactical radio communication which allows for reliable command and control, enhancing the tank's force multiplier effect on the battlefield.

Based on the lessons learned during the South African Border War with the Mk1A, the Mk1B features two drinking water tanks (one left and one right) inside the turret with a combined capacity of 101ℓ (26.8gal). The water can be accessed from the commander's and loader's station and reduces the necessity to leave the tank to fetch water. Fewer logistical tasks reduced the need for replenishment from administration and logistic support vehicles from the echelon. The addition of a fume extractor fan helps clear the interior crew compartment of excess fumes from the main gun. New and more comfortable seats were also installed to help reduce crew fatigue.

Vehicle layout

The Mk1B carried a standard complement of four crew members, consisting of the commander, gunner, loader, and driver. The commander's station is located on the right side of the turret and features a newly designed cupola, also offering a 360-degree field of vision through six vision blocks. Entry and exit from the commander's station are achieved through a hatch. On the right side of the turret, just below the commander's station is the gunner's station which is fitted with a day and night sight and to the left of the turret is the loader's station. The loader also sports a periscope for better overall situational awareness. Entry and exit for the former and latter are through the gunner's and commander's hatches and in case of emergency the loader can escape through a

hatch of his own. The driver's station received a more ergonomic overhaul, a new digital instrument panel and a yoke-type steering stick which improved comfort and reduced driver fatigue. Driver vision was improved with the addition of a third driver's periscope, thereby increasing situational awareness. The central periscope can be replaced with a passive night driving periscope allowing full day/night capability. The driver can enter and exit his station through a new single-piece hatch or in emergencies escape hatch in the floor.

Main armament

The Mk1B retained the South African produced 105mm GT3 52 calibre semi-automatic quick-firing gun manufactured by LEW. A new thermal sleeve and fume extractor help improved sustained accuracy when firing and reduce barrel droop due to heat by as much as 70-90%. The ammunition that can be used is identical to that of the Olifant Mk1A. It should be noted that the M156 HESH round is no longer used by the SANDF. Similiarly the M413 APFSDS-T is also no longer used as it was superseded by the M426/M9718 APFSDS-T. For convenience see Table 5 for the performance of each round.

Table 5: Olifant Mk1B, 105mm ammunition spesifications

105mm ammunition	Velocity	*Penetration (RHA) at zero degrees
L52A3 APDS	1,326m/s (4,350ft/s)	300mm (11.8in)
M456 HEAT	1,000m/s (3,281f/s)	420mm (16.5in)
M156 HESH	731m/s (2,398f/s)	310mm (12.2in)
M111 APFSDS-T (Fin Mk1)	1,455m/s (4,773ft/s)	390mm (15.4in)
M429 / M2A1 Mk2 APFSDS-T (Fin Mk2)	1,450m/s (4,757ft/s)	420mm (16.5in)
M426 APFSDS-T (Fin Mk3)	1,450m/s (4,757ft/s)	450mm (17.7in)
M9210 HE	700m/s (2,296ft/s)	30mm (1.2in)
M416 WP	700m/s (2,296ft/s)	N/A

★ *Penetration values are optimal at close range and decrease (except HEAT and HESH) over distance.*

The fighting compartment saw safety improvements with a total of 65 main gun rounds carried in protected stowage bins below the turret ring. The turret bustle was extended, which added more room for crew equipment and also helped balance the overall turret weight distribution, putting much less strain on the new solid-state electrical gun control system and turret drive, which can traverse the turret in a full circle in 16 seconds, an improvement of 14 seconds over the Mk1A. An infrared/white searchlight was added above the main gun.

Fire control system

In 1990 the SADF tasked Reutech Systems to develop a new FCS to replace the 30-year-old system on the Olifant Mk1A. The FCS known as the HIFF consisted of state of the art (for the time) ballistic computer system, sight drive and electronics coupled to a touch button control system and sensors which accurately measured meteorological conditions which can affect the fire accuracy of the main gun, such as ambient temperature and wind speed, from the environmental sensors. The new system allowed the gunner to select a target and in less than two seconds the FCS would calculate a fire solution and notify the gunner via a ready to fire light that the main gun was on target and ready to fire. The system can also hit a moving target while on the move itself by adjusting the main gun's aim after incorporating the target's distance, speed and relative speed, thereby maximising first-round hit probability. The gunner makes use of an Eloptro x8 gunner's day sight with an integrated ballistic computer which was added to the gunner's sight. Co-mounted is a laser range finder which is accurate up to 10km (6.2mi). Data from the rangefinder is fed into the split range drum, which applies elevation to the main gun. Tests revealed that the system is accurate within 30cm x 30 cm (11.8in x 11.8in) at 3km (1.86mi), which is perfect for the South African *"lowveld"*.

Olifant Mk1B – Nick-named Corbadus and fitted with experimental yellow test roadwheels, as seen in 1986. (G. Swart)

Olifant Mk1B – Rear view. The difference between the Mk1B and Mk2 is visible when looking at the rear hull. The Mk1B circular air outlets are visible as well as the storage bins. (Author's collection)

Protection

Having established that the Olifant Mk1A was vulnerable to the main gun of the T-54/55, T-62 and T-72M MBTs, an improvement in armour protection was required for the Mk1Bs. The Mk1B retained the original Mk1A's armour with the addition of several passive composite armour packages over the frontal glacis plate and turret (front, sides and top). The entire turret exterior was redesigned, which gave it a more modern appearance. A gap was left in between the original Mk1A turret and the add-on turret package to act as spaced armour against HEAT rounds. Additionally, this gap can be filled in the future if necessary. The total thickness of the armour package upgrade and the composition thereof is classified. However, ballistic tests showed that it provided sufficient protection to defeat 115mm HEAT rounds used by T-62 tanks. The modular add-on armour package can be replaced in the field if damaged. The entire hull can shrug off the feared 23mm anti-aircraft gunfire. Furthermore the threat posed to the Mk1A by Rocket Propelled Grenades such as the RPG-7 is negated with the mentioned upgrades to the Mk1B. The armoured steel skirts of the Mk1A were redesigned, allowing for an easier removal while still providing additional protection against RPG-7s. The constant threat of landmines in Southern Africa necessitated the addition of a double armoured floor (with the torsion bars between the floor plates). A new fire suppression system (automatic & manual) was installed in the crew and engine compartment to reduce the likelihood of a catastrophic fire or explosion if hit, in addition to a fire explosion suppression system in the turret. The storage bins received lids to reduce the chances of content ignition if the Mk1B is hit.

Olifant Mk1B Optimum – SA Armour Museum. (D. Venter)

The smoke grenade banks were prone to damage when bundu bashing, and these were therefore relocated to the rear of the turret on the Mk1B where two banks of four smoke grenade launchers were fitted. Additionally, the Mk1B can also generate a smoke screen by injecting fuel into the engine exhaust. The hull headlamps are armoured and a V-shape bush basher bar can be added to the nose of the hull. The total additional weight adds up to just over 3t.

Olifant Mk1B BLT. (Author's collection)

OLIFANT MK1B VARIANTS

Olifant Bridge Laying Tank

Although reminiscent of the Mk1B, the BLT only makes use of components and the engine found in the Mk1B. This similarity has incorrectly led some to conclude that the BLT is based on the Mk1B, which it is not. Two BLTs are employed by the SANDF Engineering Corps.

Olifant Mk1B Optimum

The Mk1B was developed as a stop-gap while the SADF was looking to acquire a brand new MBT. Project Loggim was aimed at researching, developing and manufacturing a completely domestic MBT. The technology developed for the TTD would eventually be transferred to the Mk1B Optimum in addition a new lighter turret made of advanced ceramics with a shape reminiscent of that found on the Leopard 2A4. Additionally, the Mk1B Optimum would feature rubber side plates to detonate medium HEAT rounds and at the same time, save weight. After the fall of the Soviet Union and the 1994 democratic elections, the new SANDF had a significantly reduced budget. Hence the TTD and Optimum projects were

cancelled. Most of the technologies would eventually be transferred to the Olifant Mk2.

CONCLUSION

The Mk1B was, for all practical purposes, a leap forward in protection, mobility and firepower over its predecessor, the Mk1A. However, several problems came to light, such as the poor power to weight ratio and the failure of the main gun system to exceed the performance of the Mk1A. Logistical shortcomings of parts and maintenance manuals exasperate the Mk1Bs problems. Additionally, the desired fightability improvement was not achieved. These shortcomings motivated the SANDF to look for further improvements which led to the Olifant Mk2, which made use of many of the technologies developed in the TTD.

A soldier's account – Olifant Mk1B evaluations

On E-Squadron's return from attachment to 61 Mech in South West Africa at the end of February 1986, two Olifant Mk1A crews were selected and an extra tank driver included in the group along with some Tank transporter drivers, Echelon, medic, mechanics etc and the group was attached to the Armour wing Research and Development unit under Major French and Major Wagenaar.

We travelled to Pretoria to sign secrecy documents and collected the prototype Olifant Mk1B and a standard Olifant Mk1A from OMC. The idea was to drive both vehicles in the coming months

Olifant Mk1B – E-Squadron tank crew at Vastrap 1986. (G. Swart)

through a series of trails and compare their performance. The program lasted four to five months and included tests at De Brug, Bloemfontein, Army Battle School Lohatla and Vastrap in the Northern Cape. All troops were armed with live ammo for our R5s and both tanks were transported on public roads hidden under cammo net/tarpaulins.

First stop was back in Bloemfontein, we operated from the "*Jonker Loods*" area of De Brug. Here for example we drove both tanks around the perimeter of the Debrug training area for 24 hours to measure fuel consumption, engine temperatures and compare temperatures of the standard road wheels on the Mk1A with the various synthetic materials on the Mk1B road wheels.

One lap around the training area (21km if I recall correctly) the Mk1A following the Mk1B a few kilometer[s] behind, included driving up over and down the other side of "*Stormberg*" koppie and seven laps of the tank obstacle course at flat out speed. On one of my laps around the obstacle course I managed to break a suspension unit on the Mk1B and there was at that stage only one spare. Another driver got the Mk1B right track into a trench

while turning slightly and driving at a high speed which of course pulled the right side track off…he was not popular with the tiffies!

At the end of the lap we stopped at our base of operations and the OMC guys would check and log everything, the tank would then go off on another lap and then the same would happen when the following tank arrived.

Army Battle School Lohatla we did a lot of shooting, the weapon control system was very accurate and very impressive. During Vastrap we did a lot of driving in the desert.

As operational Mk1A crews our loyalty lay with the Mk1A and we drove the guts out of that tank to try to show it was the equal of the new kid on the block Mk1B. Our Mk1A performed very well, was tough and reliable, however at the end of the day there was no doubt at all that the Mk1B outperformed it in every aspect that we were aware of!

Mk1B was more comfortable drive, significantly faster, had better ergonomics, vastly improved fire control system etc.

Trooper (retd) G.G. Swart

9

Olifant Mk2 Main Battle Tank

THE AFRICAN ELEPHANT

The Olifant Mk2 was adapted for the African battlespace based on the lessons learned from the South African Border War. It was designed and produced at a time when South Africa was no longer subject to international embargoes. Set against the backdrop of a relatively stable Southern Africa, the need for large numbers of new MBTs was put aside in favour of more agile and air-transportable vehicles for peacekeeping missions in Africa under the umbrella of the UN and AU.

DEVELOPMENT

The official planned replacement of the Olifant Mk1A was evaluated in the 1990s. Possible contenders were the French Tropicalized AMX-56 (developed for Saudi Arabia) and the British Vickers Defence Systems Challenger 2E. Initial SANF requirements asked for 96 new MBTs, six armoured recovery vehicles and four armoured vehicle-launched bridges on a similar body. However, in 1998, the South African government announced that no new MBT was to be funded for the SANDF in the foreseeable future, as the Air Force and Navy required a complete overhaul. Originally an entirely new hull would have been built, but due to a lack of funds, the only solution available to the SANDF was to upgrade the existing Mk1Bs which were on hand to the desired specifications sought by the SAAC. OMC was tasked with improving on the shortcomings of the Olifant Mk1B and this would lead to the Olifant Mk2. A total of 26 Mk2s were built from 2005 under Project Atolasa. The Mk2 is in service only with the SANDF. Four are used for training at the Army School of Armour at Tempe military base while the remaining 22 are in storage.

DESIGN FEATURES

The design, development and production of the Mk2 were undertaken to correct the shortcomings of the Mk1B. It was particularly feared that T-72M MBTs would be acquired by some of its neighbours, which would require a much more lethal South African MBT.

MOBILITY

The Mk2 would retain its predecessor's role as an MBT. The Mk2 can ford 1.5m (4.9ft) of water without preparation. With regards to the mobility, the Mk2 kept the Continental 29ℓ turbocharged V12 diesel engine of the Mk1B. Still, improvements to the engine raised the overall performance to 1,050hp (783kW), with an increase of the power-to-weight ratio from 16.1hp/t in the Mk1B to 17.35hp/t in the Mk2.

The Mk2 retained the Mk1B's automatic transmission (AMTRA 3) which was manufactured by Gear Ratio and provided double-differential steering (four forward gears and two reverse), two-speed mechanical steering drive and hydraulic

Olifant Mk2 – SA Army School of Armour, mobility course. (F. Esterhuizen)

Olifant Mk2 – De Brug Shooting Range. (J. van Zyl)

Olifant Mk2 – De Brug Shooting Range. (J. van Zyl)

retarder. The additional 190hp (142kW), coupled with the automatic transmission, allowed the Mk2 the same top speed of 58km/h (36mp/h) on road as the Mk1B, albeit accelerating 25% quicker than the Mk1B. The Mk2 also retains the Mk1B's torsion

bar suspension system with hydraulic dampers and bump stops fitted to the first and last pair of road wheels which dramatically improve off-road mobility. The overall result is a less taxing driving

Olifant Mk2 – Notice the absence of the air outlet ports at the rear compared to the Mk1B. De Brug Shooting Range. (J. van Zyl)

Olifant Mk2 – De Brug Shooting Range. (J. van Zyl)

to reduce ambient noise, thereby improving situational awareness and reducing crew fatigue.

Based on the lessons learnt during the South African Border War with the Mk1A, the Mk2 is equipped with two drinking water tanks (one left and one right) inside the turret with a combined capacity of 101ℓ (27gal). The water can be accessed from the commander's and loader's stations and reduces the necessity to leave the tank and continue water replenishment from the echelon. The addition of a fume extractor fan helped clear the interior crew compartment of excess fumes.

Vehicle layout

The Mk2 carries a standard complement of four crew, consisting of the commander, gunner, loader and driver. Further changes were made to the interior layout to enhance the ergonomics of the fighting compartment to maximise efficiency and reduce crew fatigue.

The commander's station is located on the right side of the turret and is equipped with a more modern cupola, offering a 360-degree field of vision. The commander's station also features a digital screen which

experience, especially over rough terrain. The steering of the Mk2 also remained the same as the Mk1B, which is via a yoke.

Endurance and logistics

The fuel capacity was reduced from 1,382ℓ (365gal) in the Mk1B to 1,285ℓ (339gal) in the Mk2. The reduction in fuel capacity had little impact on the overall range, and the Mk2 can travel the same distance as the Mk1B, namely 360km (224mi) on-road and 260km (162mi) off-road. Having retained the same engine as the Mk1B, no further changes were made to the size of the engine compartment. The road wheels retained the polyurethane surface, which have an operational range of 1,200km (745mi). The Mk2 also retained the same number of track links (109). The grease nipples on the road wheels were reduced from 108 in the Olifant Mk1A to 12 in the Mk2, which significantly reduced crew fatigue.

The Mk2 is equipped with one 7.62mm coaxial BMG which has a 2,000 round ready bin with 6,600 rounds of 7.62mm is carried in total. The Mk2 features tactical radio communication, allowing for reliable command and control and enhancing the tank's force multiplier effect on the battlefield. Improvements were made

is linked to the gunner's sight. The commander received a COP which is fully stabilised and equipped with thermal imaging which significantly enhances situational awareness and combat ability. The COP located on the turret roof is the most prominent feature distinguishing the Mk2 from the Mk1B. It should be noted that the COP is removed when not in operational use.

Table 6: Olifant Mk2, 105mm ammunition specifications		
Ammunition 105mm	**Velocity**	***Penetration (RHA) at zero degrees**
M456 HEAT	1,000m/s (3,281f/s)	420mm (16.5 in)
M111 APFSDS-T (Fin Mk1)	1,455m/s (4,773ft/s)	390mm (15.4 in)
M426 APFSDS-T (Fin Mk3)	1,450m/s (4,757ft/s)	450mm (17.7 in)
M9210 HE	700m/s (2,296ft/s)	30mm (1.2in)
M416 WP	700m/s (2,395ft/s)	N/A

* *Penetration values are optimal at close range and decrease (except HEAT) over distance.*

On the right side of the turret, below the commander's station, is the gunner's station which is equipped with day/night capabilities that are displayed on a digital screen. The loader also has an episcope for better situational awareness. Entry and exit for the former and latter are through the commander's hatch and, in case of emergency, the loader can escape through a hatch above his station.

The driver's station retained the ergonomic overhaul, digital instrument panel and a yoke-type steering stick from the Mk1B, which improved comfort and reduced driver fatigue. Driver vision is through three episcopes, allowing better vision, thereby increasing situational awareness. The central episcope can be replaced with a passive night driving periscope allowing full night capability. The driver can enter and exit his station through a single-piece hatch above his station while an emergency escape hatch is located under the seat in the floor.

Main armament

The Mk2 retained the South African produced 105mm GT3 52 calibre semi-automatic quick-firing gun manufactured by LEW and the standard thermal sleeve and fume extractor upgrade given to the Mk1B. As with the Mk1B the Mk2 can shoot the same 105mm ammunition as the Mk1A. For convenience see Table 6 for the performance of each round. The M111 APFSDS-T (Fin Mk1) is used for training while the newer M426 APFSDS-T (Fin Mk3) is kept in strategic reserve. The locally design and manufactured M9210 HE is also still used.

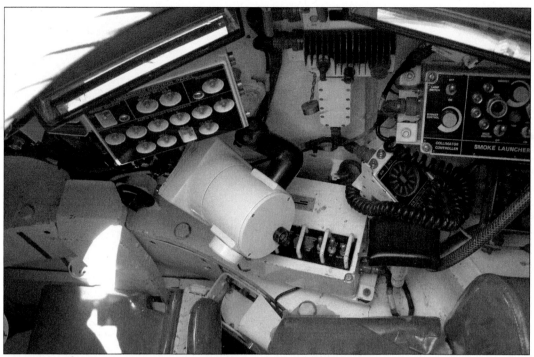

Olifant Mk2 – AAD 2012. Crew commander's station from above. On the right is the smoke launcher control panel, and interior turret lights. Just below is the traverse indicator. On the right is the crew commander's gunnery control, traverse turret, aim barrel, laser range finder, stabiliser control and fire button. On the top left is the crew commander gunnery control panel. (S. Tegner)

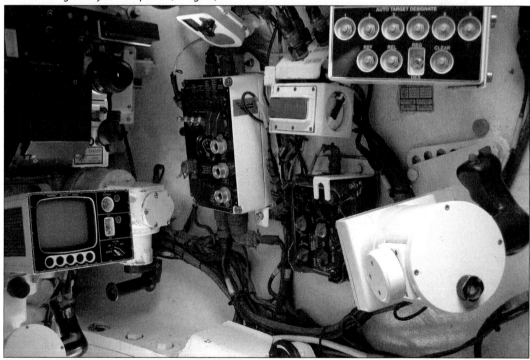

Olifant Mk2 – AAD 2012. Gunner station right hand side. On the turret wall to the right is the radio box. To the left is the gunner control box with the covered switches used to activate the fire suppression system. Above the aforementioned is the turret light with two settings, white light day and green light evening. The screen is the gunnery computer and to the right is the manual turret traverse wheel. Below the screen is the gunner's fire, turret and barrel control for stabilised firing. Above the screen to the right is the gunner's main sight. (S. Tegner)

The fighting compartment saw safety improvements with a total of 64 main gun rounds carried, some in protected stowage bins below the turret ring, while a number are kept in ready bins for immediate use. The extended bustle (compared to the Olifant Mk1A) not only allowed for more room for crew equipment but also helped balance the overall turret weight distribution. This, in turn, puts far less strain on the new solid-state electrical gun control system and turret drive which can traverse the turret a full 360 degrees in 16 seconds.

Fire control system

The Mk2 features a wholly integrated FCS. The FCS allows the gunner or commander to target an enemy which engages the auto-tracking feature to keep the main gun on target while the tank is moving. The gunner makes use of a digital display screen to select a target and which displays the results of the integrated ballistic

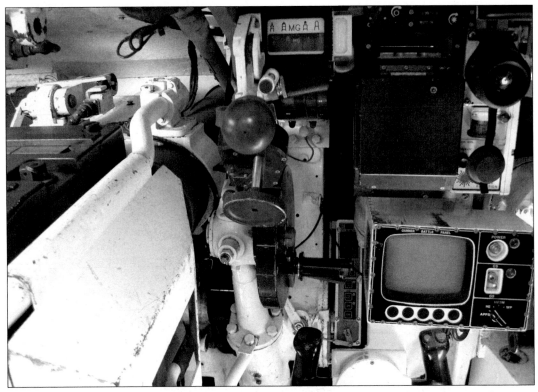

Olifant Mk2 – AAD 2012. Gunner station left hand side. The knob in the centre is used to adjust the range drum. At the top are the different calibrations for the different rounds possible. Below the knob is the manual elevation wheel. The gun breech is on the left. (S. Tegner)

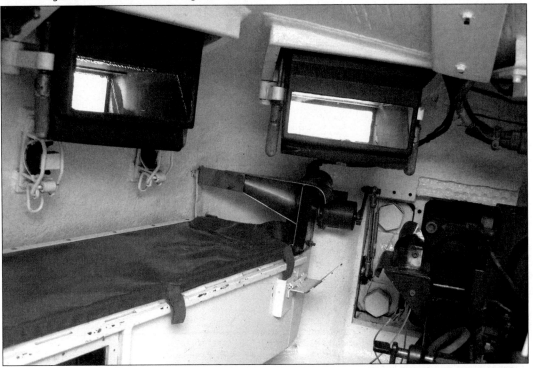

Olifant Mk2 – AAD 2012. Loader station. On the left is where the 7.62mm ammunition is kept for the coaxial BMG. On the right is the housing for the BMG. On the top left is the loader's periscopes. (S. Tegner)

engaging an enemy first. The commander can override the gunner's aim with the flip of a switch to put the main cannon on target. A well-trained crew can lase a target, load the main gun round and fire every eight seconds.

Protection

The Mk2's armour is the same as the Mk1B and consists of the original Centurion Mk5's armour of 76mm (2.99in) on the frontal glacis at 58 degrees, 152mm frontal turret (6in), 51mm (2in) on the sides, 40mm (1.57in) on top and 29mm (1.14in) in the rear of the tank. An armour upgrade program took the form of several passive composite armour packages, one over the frontal glacis plate and several on the turret (front, sides and top). A gap was left between the original Centurion turret and the added armour package to act as spaced armour. The total thickness and composition of these armour packages are classified. However, it has been publicly stated that the Mk2's frontal armour can stop a 115mm HEAT round as used by the T-62 tank.

The entire hull can shrug off the feared 23mm AP rounds. The threat posed to the Olifant Mk1A by RPG-7 is negated with the mentioned upgrades to the Mk2 armour. Additionally, the armoured steel skirts of the Mk1A were redesigned for the Mk2 to protect the running gear from incoming missiles by prematurely detonating incoming HEAT rounds. The constant threat of landmines in Southern Africa necessitated the addition of a double armoured floor (with the torsion bars

computer. The laser rangefinder is integrated into the system and is accurate to up to 10km (6.2mi). Data from the rangefinder is by design fed into an integrated ballistic computer, which applied elevation to the main gun. Tests revealed that the system was accurate within 30cm x 30 cm (11.8in x 11.8in) at 2km (1.24mi) which was sufficient for the South African "lowveld".

An additional feature that makes the Mk2 lethal is its hunter-killer capability. This allows the commander and gunner to independently scan for targets, thereby maximising the chance of spotting and

between the floor plates). A new fire suppression system (automatic and manual) was installed in the crew and engine compartment to reduce the likelihood of a catastrophic fire or explosion if hit.

The Mk2 has two banks of four smoke grenade launchers fitted to the rear of the turret, which lessens the possibility of damage when bundu bashing. Additionally, the Mk2 can also generate a smoke screen by injecting fuel into the engine exhaust. The hull headlamps are armoured, and a V-shape bush basher bar can be added to the nose of the hull.

CONCLUSION

The Mk2 addresses the shortcomings initially found in the Mk1B to make the tank fightable by incorporating the hunter-killer capability. Furthermore, a more powerful engine improves the tank's overall performance. The Mk2 is a leap forward in protection, mobility and firepower and is currently the pinnacle of tank technology in Southern Africa. The role of MBTs is essentially to act as a deterrent to outside aggressors. MBTs are prohibitively expensive to operate and maintain, and as they are often only deployed during times of war this makes the justification for funding them very difficult to the general public. The South African defence industry's ingenuity has stretched the life expectancy of the Olifant MBT impressively. It should, however,

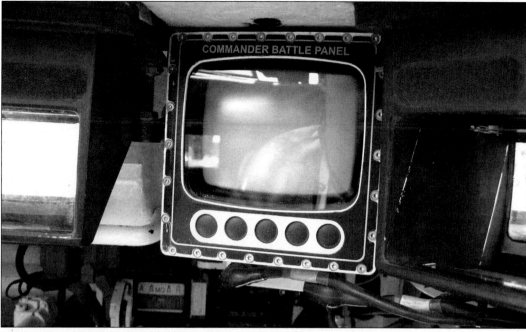

Olifant Mk2 – AAD 2012. Crew commander station. Battle panel displays a thermal image from the COP sight. (S. Tegner)

be noted that the fleet needs to be replaced as the hulls are nearing 50 years of age.

10

Tank Technology Demonstrator

THE TANK THAT COULD HAVE BEEN

Years of technological development in South Africa culminated in a locally-built prototype MBT called the 'Tank Technology Demonstrator'. Initially developed while there was a perceived external threat, the TTD served as a testbed for the most modern technologies of the time in the areas of firepower, mobility, and survivability. According to the then Defence Minister Kobie Coetsee (1993-1994), the tank compared well with overseas systems such as the Leopard 2 and American Abrams.

DEVELOPMENT

The SADF identified, in the early 1980s, the need for an entirely new generation of indigenous MBTs. This project, code-named *Loggim*, was assigned to the Reumech Olifant Manufacturing Company (OMC), which produced the hull, and Lyttleton Engineering Works (LEW), which designed the turret and main gun. Other companies involved in the project were Kentron (which later became Denel Dynamics), integrators of Systems Technology (iST) (now IST Dynamics), Grinaker Electronics, Eloptro (specialists in optics), Booyco Engineering (air conditioning systems for armoured vehicles), M-TEK (specialists in the design, development, control and manufacture of precision electro-mechanical components and sub-systems), Prokura Diesel Services (PDS) (supply or develop power packs for armoured vehicles).

With the end of the South African Border War, defence spending was no longer a priority and funding was cut for the project in the early 1990s. Not wanting the technological advancements and effort go to waste, the SADF and the ARMSCOR decided to produce

one vehicle to showcase the TTD's potential capability and serve as a development platform. The TTD was completed in 1992 and was intended to replace the Olifant Mk1B.

By 1994, South Africa held its first free democratic elections. Subsequently, sanctions were lifted, and South Africa was again allowed to purchase and sell arms on the international market. It was argued by the SANDF that a modern MBT could just as easily be purchased from an international supplier and at a far more competitive price than it would be to build locally. The TTD served as a culmination of all the technological research and industrial capacity available in South Africa during the early 1990s with subsequent comparisons to be made with other MBTs of the era. At the time of its development, the chief opposing MBT was considered the T-72M with its 125mm main gun. It can be argued that, if the decision was taken to produce the new MBT, the final variant would have been strikingly similar to the TTD. It was envisaged that 282 of these MBTs would be built on the completion of the project in order to replace the Olifant Mk1A and Mk1B.

With the subsequent cancellation of the MBT project and no acquisition on the table, the TTD was donated to the South African Armour Museum in 1996/7.

DESIGN FEATURES

The design, development, and production of the TTD were undertaken to showcase what would be possible if an indigenous MBT was produced. The TTD design made it easily possible to optimise the vehicle according to mission requirements, as subsystems can be tailor-made.

TTD – SA Army School of Armour. (SA Army Armour Formation)

TTD – Military exercise. (SA Army Armour Formation)

to reduce power output to protect the powerpack, which subsequently aids in increasing its service life.

The engine is driven through an automatic 4F 2R cross drive gearbox with four forward and two reverse gears. The final drives incorporate a planetary gear reduction with an offset configuration which can handle up to 1,500hp (1,120kW) at 1200rpm. With fuel efficiency in mind, the powerpack would switch from eight to four cylinders when the TTD stood still. The steering allows the TTD to pivot turn and is infinitely variable for large, fixed and tight turns. A turning circle at low speed is 15m (49ft) and 36m (118ft) at high speed.

The suspension consists of a torsion bar with friction rotary dampers, and hydraulic bump stops and makes use of live track which produces lower noise and lower transmission vibration which in turn provides more stabilised fire while on the move. The live track runs over seven rubber-tired dual road wheels with a front idler, a rear driving sprocket and four return rollers. The TTD's ground pressure is 0.93kg/cm² (32.8oz/cm²). The TTD can climb a gradient of 60%, a side slope of 30% and can cross a 3.5m (11.5ft) trench. Unprepared, the TTD can ford 1.5m (4.9ft) of water.

Mobility

One of the critical design requirements of the TTD was that it had to be able to self-deploy quickly via road over distance if transporters were not available. The TTD is powered by a twin-turbo intercooled V-8 diesel engine that delivers 1,234hp (920kW) at 1,200rpm. This translates into a power-to-weight ratio of 21.16hp/t. The maximum torque that can be produced is 4,400Nm at 1,500rpm, which allows the TTD to accelerate from 0-30km/h (0-18.6mph) within 5.1sec. It has a top speed of 71km/h (44mph) on road and 35km/h (22mph) off-road.

The engine is cooled by a water-to-air system which involves splitting the air and water to the intake manifold. Additionally, the warm exhaust gasses are mixed with the cooled air to reduce the TTD's IR signature. Doing so makes the TTD less visible to enemies using IR vision which detects thermal energy. The power pack is equipped with a Management System which regulates the power output at 100% at ambient temperatures of up to 48°C (118 °F). Higher temperatures require the Management System

The TTD has a minimum of 102 and a maximum of 112 track links, depending on the required track tension. The road wheels are mounted on a torsion bar system with 500mm (19.7in) of vertical travel (320mm [12.6in] up and 180mm [7in] down). The impact energy on the road wheels is absorbed by wear-resistant, maintenance-free hydraulic variable-resistance friction dampers and hydraulic bump stops. The braking system is integrated into the gearbox and comprises a primary retarder and double disc brakes. This allows the TTD to come to a complete halt from 56km/h (35mph) in 6.8sec. The resulting heat generated by the friction is dispersed through the brakes' air-cooled system. In case an emergency engine start is required, a hydraulic start system is incorporated should the electrical one or the starter fail.

Endurance and logistics

Another key design requirement was that the TTD had to be able to operate far away from any workshop support and was to be maintained by reservists. The TTD has a 1,600ℓ (422gal) diesel fue tank which gives it a road range of 400km (249mi) at 50km/h (31mph). Off-road range is 300km (186mi) at 35km/h (22mph). On sand, the range is reduced to 150km (93mi). The TTD has a maximum reverse speed of 32km/h (20mph). The TTD featured the most modern tactical radio communication equipment of the time, which allowed for reliable command and control, enhancing the tank's force multiplier effect on the battlefield. The overall interior design assisted in reducing ambient noise, thereby improving situational awareness and reducing crew fatigue. The TTD is fitted with a 7.62mm coaxial BMG which is fed from a 2,000 ready round bin.

Additionally, a 7.62mm BMG can be fitted to the roof. The tank is equipped with an 80ℓ (20gal) internal drinking water tank for the crew which can be accessed at the loader's and driver's stations. A fume extractor fan helps clear the interior crew compartment of excess fumes produced when firing the main gun.

TTD – Public display Bloemfontein. (SA Army Armour Formation)

TTD – SA Armour Musuem. (J. van Zyl)

Vehicle layout

The TTD carries a standard complement of four crewmen, consisting of the commander, gunner, loader, and driver. The fighting compartment was designed with ergonomics in mind, which would maximise efficiency and reduce crew fatigue. The commander's station is located on the right side of the turret and is equipped with a sunken cupola which offered a 360-degree field of vision through six periscopes. The sunken cupola reduced the overall height of the vehicle as well as the chance that a partial hit can deflect into the crew compartment. The commander's station consists of traditional mechanical sights. It was, however, planned that digital screens be installed at a later point, which would have linked to the gunner's sight. The commander has at his disposal a CS60N primary stabilized commander's sight offering a 360-degree panoramic detection, recognition and identification view via a periscope in the cupola, which has x3 and x10 magnification options. It features a two-axis, gyro-stabilized mirror head. Additionally, a 3rd generation image intensifier night channel is incorporated, which significantly enhances situational awareness and combat ability in low-light conditions. The MBT variant would have seen a thermal imaging intensifier added.

Just below the commander's station, on the right side of the turret, is the gunner's station, which is equipped with a day/night capabilities. This station would also have received digital display screens if the final MBT variant had been built. Entry and exit for the commander and gunner are through the commander's hatch. The loader's station is on the left side of the turret and has a dedicated episcope for better situational awareness. Entry and exit for the loader are through his own dedicated hatch.

The driver's station features an ergonomic design, with an analogue instrument panel and a yoke-type steering stick which improved comfort and reduced driver fatigue. The driver's station would also have received a digital screen overhaul in the final MBT version. The driver makes use of three episcopes, allowing better vision, thereby increasing situational awareness. The central episcope can be replaced with a passive night driving periscope allowing full night capability. The driver can enter and exit his station through a single-piece hatch above the station while an emergency escape hatch is located underneath the seat in the floor.

Main armament

For testing purposes, the TTD is fitted with a standard 105mm GT3 52 calibre semi-automatic quick-firing gun developed by LEW in South Africa. The 52 calibre barrel is rifled and is encased in a thermal shield. A total of 54 main gun rounds is carried, of which six are kept in the turret basket, 16 in the turret bustle and 32 in the ammunition racks to the left of the driver.

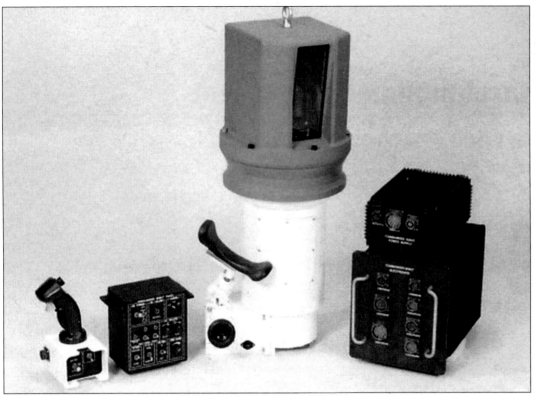

CS60N commander's sight. (Denel marketing poster)

The breech slides horizontally and is semi-automatic. Tests revealed that first-round hit probability of a T-72 sized target at 2km (1.2mi) is higher than 84% while static and 75% while in motion.

The gun drive makes use of a 48V compact brushless DC motor, two pinion azimuth drive and linear extension elevation drive. The azimuth drive can rotate the turret a full 360 degrees in less than 10 seconds with an acceleration of 0.6rad/s. Elevation speed and acceleration are rated at 0.6rad/s. Also included is a two-axis primary stabilized GS60 gunner sight with an x3 and x8 magnification. Additionally, a laser rangefinder with a 200–8,000m (218-8,749 yard) range is integrated together with a 120 element thermal imager which is projected on monitors at both the commander and gunner stations. The gunner also has at his disposal a mechanical telescopic auxiliary backup sight.

The main gun ammunition is stored in the turret and floor. The ready rounds are stored on the turret floor and turret bustle via a loading port. Ammunition is provided by a rotating carousel which supplies ammunition to the loader who can load between six and eight rounds a minute.

Fire control system

The FCS makes use of an RS485 serial databus linking all the sub-systems to allow for effective hunter-killer mode, allowing the gunner and commander to hunt for enemy targets independently. Once a target has been identified, the main gun is slaved on to the target by the gunner or by the commander with an override facility. The fire directing system makes use of a compact 48VDC electro-mechanical gun drive with a fully-integrated digital FCS. Reaction time from target acquisition to round on target is less than nine seconds. The FCS calculates ballistic offsets and improves first-round hit probability by incorporating the TTD's tilt angle and forward speed, the target moving speed, crosswind, barometric pressure, outside temperature, ammunition temperature, and target distance drop and flight speed. Additionally, the incorporated muzzle reference system allows for more accurate gun calibration. The FCS computes a ballistic calculation in 0.01mrad and has a cycle time of 5ms.

Protection

The TTD's passive armour comprises of multiple layers of spaced armour with the effective thickness of the frontal glacis offering the equivalent of protection of 750mm (29.5in) RHA. The turret thickness and composition are classified. Both the frontal hull and turret are said to protect against 125mm APFSDS and HEAT rounds. The crew and critical subsystems are protected against 23mm AP round attacks from the flanks and rear, the top armour is rated against 155mm air-burst rounds and the bottom hull is

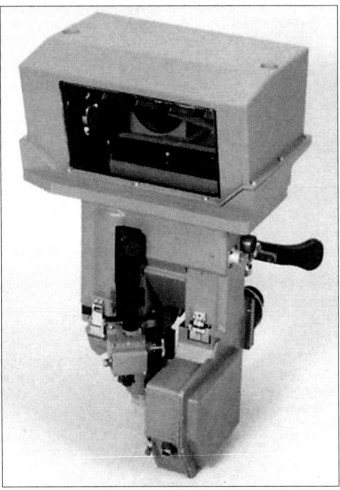

GS60 Primary stabilized gunner sight. (Denel marketing poster)

The PPM gun would have been a LEW 120mm smoothbore weapon or as part of its planned upgrade evolution a 140mm smoothbore gun. According to sources, three 120mm main guns were built. The main gun can depress -10 degrees and elevate 20 degrees.

LEW 120mm smooth-bore gun – Testing for the TTD. (Author's collection)

rated against anti-tank mine blasts under a track. Additional reactive armour packages were to be added to the turret and hull to counter anti-tank missiles.

The TTD's onboard fire explosion suppression system is automatically activated by optical detectors which are fitted in the turret and driver's compartment. Should an explosion occur in the turret bustle magazine, blow off panels allow the explosive energy to be directed outwards, thereby reducing the risk to the crew. The crew compartment is also isolated from the bustle, thereby maximising survivability in case of a hit on the bustle.

The engine compartment has its own dedicated fire extinguishing system which activates automatically when a fire is detected. The system can also be activated manually. The fuel tank is filled with *"Explosafe"* which prevents the formation of destructive pressure after the ignition of vapours or gases.

The TTD has biological and chemical protection via seals and an overpressure system at 600 Pa in addition to an air filtration system. The interior ergonomics allow for individual crew Biological-Chemical protection as well. Crew comfort in warm weather conditions is assured through an internal cooling system which consists of 12kW macro and 5kW micro cooling, which enhances crew durability.

The interior of the TTD is fully lined with an anti-spalling layer to reduce the chance of ricocheting shrapnel. The integrated cooling measure significantly reduces the TTD's exterior IR signature. On either side of the turret, behind a sheet of armour, is a bank of four 81mm smoke grenade launchers. The TTD is fitted with an exhaust smoke generating system.

CONCLUSION

Lt Col. C. Klopper of the SA Army Armour Formation, Research and Development summarises the TTD as follows:

TTD consisted of a well-advanced suspension, tracks and drive lines that were very much based on the Leopard 2 suspension. The gun drive system and to a lesser extent, the power pack did have certain shortcomings. The power pack was [an] MTU ship generator engine which generates 1234hp (920kW) at 1200rpm. This engine was upgraded and modified intensively for military use to deliver optimal output for this specific application. The transmission will be obsolete in the modern environment of MBTs. The turret did experience certain shortcomings with a sub-

standard stabilizing system, with a 1.2 mills standard deviation. The acceptable standard deviation specification is 0.4 mills or better. The FCS is inferior to the current world trend and not completely developed to its full potential. It can be believed that the TTD was much superior regarding its suspension, drive lines and power pack; however, the gun drive and FCS did not meet specifications and expectations. I am of the opinion that TTD can still be a factor on the modern battlefield with the upgrade of its FCS and gun drive system.

The TTD embodied the most sophisticated technologies, technical expertise, and manufacturing capabilities available to South Africa in the mid-1990s. With the cancellation of the project and no orders placed for a new MBT by the SANDF, the TTD was donated to the SA Armour Museum where it is on display. In 1998, the South African government announced that no new MBT was to be funded in the foreseeable future, as the Air Force and Navy required a complete overhaul. This announcement sparked some heated concerns from South Africa's neighbours. It can be argued that, if the envisaged 282 new MBTs were ordered domestically, their strategic influence on Southern Africa would have been significant and could very well have sparked a regional arms race. Between 2000 and 2005 South Africa upgraded 26 of its Olifant Mk1B to Mk2 standard which makes extensive use of various TTD subsystems.

11

Rooikat Armoured Car

THE AFRICAN CARACAL

The Rooikat armoured car takes its Afrikaans name from the African Caracal a type of wild cat. Similar to its namesake, the Rooikat armoured car is fast and nimble, being used by the SADF and its successor, the SANDF. The Rooikat is a completely indigenous military vehicle, adapted for the Southern African battlespace. This was set against the backdrop of the Cold War in Southern Africa, which saw a steep rise in liberation movements backed by Eastern Bloc communist countries such as Cuba and the Soviet Union.

DEVELOPMENT

The SADF relied heavily on the Eland 90 armoured car during the mid-1970s and early 1980s conventional battles of the South African Border War, such as Operation Savannah. Although successfully used in combat, the Eland 90's poor power to weight ratio resulted in poor forward acceleration. This resulted in it lagging behind the more powerful Ratel ICVs with which it was supposed to operate. What was required was a domestically-built armoured car suited to the Southern African battlespace which necessitates long-range strategic mobility.

The development of the Rooikat was one of South Africa's most ambitious undertakings, with the project approval for a new generation armoured car being granted in 1974. The user requirements were completed in November 1976, after which ARMSCOR began compiling technical specifications which led to several research studies of 6×6 and 8×8 configurations by South African manufacturers. A decision was made in August of 1978 that three prototypes would be built to evaluate, amongst others, the suspensions. All three were delivered in 1979. Although the decision to adopt a naval 76/62mm main gun had already been taken in 1978, all the prototypes were fitted with a British 77mm Mk2 gun from retired South African Comet tanks. The three prototypes were based on and modified from existing hulls used in the SADF, namely the Ratel ICV (Concept 1), Eland armoured car (Concept 2) and Saracen APC (Concept 3) and were of 8×8 configuration. None of the three prototypes was deemed suitable after trials held in 1979 and the project was put on ice.

The staff requirement for the new generation armoured car was put forward in 1980. Three new prototypes were built by Sandock Austral for trials which were held in March 1982. The prototypes were divided into a light, medium and heavy class (1-3). The Class 1 prototype, nicknamed Cheetah Mk1, was built according to the required light specifications which were for a 17t vehicle in a 6×6 configuration and mounting a 76mm high-pressure main gun turret. It featured basic protection to increase power to weight ratio. The Class 2 prototype came in two variants, 2A and 2B. The Class 2A's engine was located in the front which left sufficient space at the rear to be used as a troop compartment. The Class 2B had a traditional layout with the engine mounted in the rear. The Class 2B was nicknamed Cheetah Mk2 and was built according to the required medium specifications which were for a 23t vehicle in an 8×8 configuration with a 76mm high-pressure main gun turret. The Class 3 prototype, nicknamed Bismarck, was built according to the required heavy specifications, which were for a 30t vehicle in 8×8 configuration with a 105mm L7 main gun turret.

After the trials, the Class 2B prototype was selected for further development and manufacturing. In 1986/7, Sandock Boksburg completed an additional five advanced development models. Four of these were used for operational testing and assessment by the SADF in 1987 and christened the Rooikat armoured car, while the remaining two were divided between ARMSCOR and Ermetek for testing and development. By late 1988, three more Rooikats were delivered in conjunction with 23 PPM. The first SADF Rooikat squadron was delivered to 1 SSB in mid-August 1989.

Full production of the Rooikat began in June 1990 and lasted until 2000. Production was done in a series of four lots. The first lot consisted of the 28 PPM, the second (Mk1A), third (Mk1B) and fourth (Mk1C) lot each consisted of a regiment of 72 Rooikat armoured cars. With each progressive production lot after the first, slight improvements were made as indicated by their mark designation. A total of 214 Rooikat armoured cars was produced by 2000, which brought the total to 242. LEW, a world leader in combat reconnaissance turrets was responsible for the design development and building of the Rooikat turrets. Several subcontractors were involved

Rooikat 76Mk1D – On exercise. (F. Esterhuizen)

such as Eloptro who supplied the optical equipment for the turret while Kentron manufactured the gyros for the stabilisation system. Sandock Austral was responsible for the design, development, and building of the Rooikat hull and system integration. A performance and reliability enhancement programme was launched in 2000 under Project Arum Lily and lasted until 2006 which saw 80 Rooikat armoured cars being upgraded from the Mk1C to Mk1D standard, which is the most modern variant.

The Rooikat armoured car was designed with an emphasis on mobility. Firepower was the second most important feature. Protection was the least important as additional armour would have come at the cost of mobility. The principal tasks of the Rooikat as set out by the SADF included combat reconnaissance, seek and destroy operations, combat support, anti-armour and anti-guerrilla operations. Present SANDF doctrine places emphasis during combat operations on combat reconnaissance, harassment of enemy concentrations and rearguard units, disruption of enemy cohesion, logistical centres and supply trains and attacking targets of opportunity. During peacekeeping operations, the Rooikat can be used to monitor ceasefires, protect key points, escort convoys, act as a deterrent, and be used for reconnaissance and crowd control. In total, the SADF took delivery of 242 Rooikat armoured cars.

Presently, there are 80 Mk1D Rooikat armoured cars in service with the SANDF while a further 92 remain in storage. The Rooikat is assigned to the SA Army School of Armour and 1 SSB at Tempe military base in Bloemfontein. In addition, three Reserve Force units are also allocated Rooikat armoured cars, namely Umvoti Mounted Rifles in Durban, Regiment Oranjerivier in Cape Town and Regiment Mooirivier in Potchefstroom.

Concept 1 – Based on the Ratel ICV. (D. Venter)

Concept 2 – Based on the Eland AC Car. (D. Venter)

Concept 3 – Based on the Saracen APC. (D. Venter)

DESIGN FEATURES

The design, development, and production of the Rooikat were undertaken due to the increasing need for a purpose-built armoured

Class 1 prototype – Based on the Henschel Wehrtechnik TH-400. (D. Venter)

Class 2C prototype – Classified as medium. (D. Venter)

required less maintenance than a tracked vehicle. The Rooikat has a hydro-mechanical, manual shift, drop-down gearbox. The gear selection range consists of six forward, a neutral and one reverse gear. The Rooikat can ford 1m of water without preparation and 1.5m (4.9ft) with preparation. The Rooikat is powered by a twin-turbocharged, water-cooled, 10-cylinder Atlantis diesel engine fitted with an intercooler which can produce 563hp (420kW). This provides a 20.1hp/t power to weight ratio. The Rooikat Mk1D can accelerate from 0-60km/h (0-37mph) in 21 seconds and can achieve a maximum road speed of 120km/h (75mph), with a safe cruising speed of 90km/h (90mph). Changes were made to the engine from the Mk1C to the Mk1D, which involved better connection points which improved the overall reliability of the engine. Due to the dusty conditions in Southern Africa, the engine has a primary and secondary dust filter. A 2m (6.6ft) wide ditch can be crossed at a crawl. The Rooikat is capable of retaining mobility even with just one steerable wheel on either side.

The Rooikat is equipped with fully independent, internally driven trailing arms, coil springs, and shock-absorbers. The driver makes use of a power-assisted steering wheel which controls the front four wheels and foot pedals for acceleration and braking. The Rooikat has a ground clearance of 380mm (15in) and 350mm (13in) with the addition of a mine protection plate.

Endurance and logistics

The fuel capacity of the Rooikat is 540ℓ (143gal) which allows it to travel 1,000km (621mi) on road, 500km (311mi) off-road and 150km (93mi) over sand on a single tank. The Rooikat Mk1C was equipped with two 7.62mm belt-fed machine guns with a total of 3,800 rounds. One machine gun was co-axially mounted on the left side of the main gun while the other was located on top of the turret structure above the commander's station for close protection against ground and air threats. The Mk1D saw the removal of the second machine gun. The Rooikat is fitted with very high-frequency tactical communication radios which allow for reliable inter-crew communication, command and control which enhances the armoured car's force multiplier effect on the battlefield. The

car which was suited for the Southern African battlespace. Furthermore, there was a dire need for an armoured car which could keep up with mechanised formations. The terrain it would operate in would be some of the most hostile in the world, which alone inflicts harsh punishment. Characterised by its eight massive wheels, mobility, bush breaking ability and versatility as a weapons platform, the Rooikat is well adapted for its role as a modern armoured car.

The Rooikat would be pushed into service because it can outmanoeuvre and attack tanks in battle conditions common to southern Africa, where engagements often are at close quarters.

Lt. Gen. Andreas (Kat) Liebenberg (1988), chief of the Army

Mobility

The Southern African battlespace favours a wheeled configuration, in which the Rooikat's 8×8 configuration excels. An eight-wheel 16:00x20 run-flat configuration offered more reliability and

Class 2B prototype – Classified as medium. (D. Genis)

Class 3 prototype – Based on the Henschel Wehrtechnik TH-800. (SA Armour Museum)

Class 3 prototype – With an Olifant Mk1B turret. (D. Venter)

ability to override the gunner's control and slave the main gun onto a target via the panoramic sight, which is coupled to the integrated FCS. This allows for extreme accuracy and quick reaction times.

On the right side of the turret, below the commander's station, is the gunner's station which is equipped with day/night capabilities that are displayed on a digital display screen.

On the left side of the turret is the loader's station. The loader has access to two periscopes, one facing forward and the other facing aft; both fitted on the left-hand side of the turret roof structure which can each rotate 270-degrees for better overall situational awareness. Entry and exit for the loader are via a single-piece hatch. In case of emergency, the loader, gunner and commander can escape through service hatches located on either side of the hull between the second and third wheel.

The driver's station is situated in the front centre of the hull and is accessible through the fighting compartment or a single-piece hatch above the driver's station. The driver's station is fully adjustable and features three periscopes for enhanced vision and situational awareness. The central periscope can be replaced with a passive night driving periscope (manufactured by Eloptro) allowing full day/night capability. Making use of compressed air the driver can clean his periscopes while closed down. The ergonomic

Rooikat features a built-in drinking water tank with a 40ℓ (10.6gal) water capacity accessible on the outside of the hull on the left.

design and layout of the equipment in each section allows the crew to work fast and accurately under stressful battle conditions.

Vehicle layout

The Rooikat carries a standard complement of four crew members, consisting of the commander, gunner, loader, and driver. The commander's station is located on the right side of the turret and features a 360-degree field of vision through eight vision blocks which provide all-round vision. Forward of the commander's station on the roof structure is a day panoramic sight which allows the commander a 360-degree x12 magnification capability without the need to move his head. Additionally, the commander has the

Main armament

The main armament is a South African GT4 76mm quick-firing semi-automatic gun manufactured by LEW. The main gun is a derivative of the Italian Otobreda 76mm compact naval gun and has the same chamber volume. The APFSDS-T round consisting of a tungsten alloy penetrator has a muzzle velocity of over 1,600m/s and is capable of penetrating 311mm (12in) of RHA at 10m (32.8ft). This allows the Rooikat to penetrate the front hull (275mm [10.8 in]) and turret (230mm [9 in]) of a T-62 MBT at 2km (1.24mi). The

Rooikat 76 Mk1D – Public display. (R. Fouche)

APFSDS-T weighs in at 9.1kg (20lb) and is 87.3cm (34in) long. The HE-T round carries 0.6kg (1.3lb) of RDX/TNT, can penetrate 20mm (0.8in) of RHA and has an effective range of 3km (1.86mi) when used in direct fire and 12km (7.45mi) in the indirect fire role. Canister ammunition can be used effectively at up to 150m (164 yd) with a high probability of killing and up to 500m (547yd) with a high degree of maiming. The gun barrel is equipped with a thermal anti-distortion sleeve and reinforced fibreglass fume extractor which helps improve sustained accuracy when firing and reduces barrel droop due to heat.

Rooikat 76 Mk1C engine – SA Army School of Armour. (D. Venter)

The standard rate of fire for the main gun either stationary or at a short halt is six rounds a minute. The turret drive can traverse the turret a full 360 degrees in 9 seconds. The main gun can elevate from -10 degrees to +20 degrees. Making use of a 76mm main gun instead of a 105mm has several advantages. It allows for a higher number of rounds to be carried (49 vs 36) which allows for more engagements, reduced weight, less recoil force (320mm [12.6in] vs 350mm [13.78in]) which means a smaller turret and greater negative elevation, higher rate of fire, better ergonomics and faster turret rotation speed. These advantages facilitate the Rooikat's role in combat reconnaissance, seek and destroy operations and harassing enemy rearguard units. The fighting compartment of the Mk1D can carry a total of 49 main gun rounds of which nine are ready rounds stowed vertically below the turret ring.

Fire control system

The gunner makes use of an Eloptro x8 gunner's day sight with an integrated ballistic computer which was added to the gunner's sight. The IFCS produced by ESD receives information from the laser rangefinder and environmental sensors which accurately measure meteorological conditions such as ambient temperature and wind speed which can affect the fire accuracy of the main gun rounds. Such variations are automatically calculated and compensated for in conjunction with the ammunition selected and fed into the gunner's sights and main gun's auto lay aim. The IFCS can achieve a hit on a moving target by adjusting the main gun's aim after incorporating the target's distance, speed and relative speed, thereby maximising first-round hit probability. From the moment the gunner selects a target, the IFCS produces a fire solution within two seconds. When the main gun is ready, the gunner is notified via a "ready to fire" light. The entire engagement process takes roughly nine seconds. The development of the solid-state gun drive systems by ESD as part

Rooikat 105. (Denel marketing poster)

MTTD – With a 105 auto loader turret. (D. Venter)

manual) was installed in the crew and engine compartment to reduce the likelihood of a catastrophic fire or explosion if hit.

Lessons learned during the South African Border War showed that smoke grenade banks were prone to damage when bundu bashing, which necessitated the placement thereof to the rear sides of the turret. A bank of four electrically operated 81mm smoke grenade launchers located on the side of the turret are used for self-screening in an emergency. The Rooikat is also fitted with an instantaneous smoke emission system that can produce a smoke screen by injecting fuel into the engine exhaust at the rear left of the hull. The operation of the screen is controlled by the driver. The frontal headlamps are under armoured covers to protect against damage. The Rooikat is also capable of full NBC protection but is not fitted as standard.

ROOIKAT FAMILY
Rooikat 105

In an attempt to up-gun the Rooikat for the international market which included the UAE and Oman, Reumeck OMC and LEW created a variant with a GT-7 105mm (52-calibre) gun, with development completed in 1994. The Rooikat 105 shared the same general design as the Rooikat 76, only differing in the larger calibre gun and modernised FCS. Being

of the Reutech Group was a big step forward for the SA Armoured Corps as it brought fire-on-the-move capabilities to Rooikat.

Protection

The Rooikat's hull is made of all-welded steel armour and is sufficient to afford all-round protection against shrapnel and small arms fire from close range. Over the entire 30 degrees frontal arc, the Rooikat is protected against 23mm armour-piercing projectiles fired from medium range (+500m\+546yd) while the sides and rear offer protection against 12.7mm AP rounds. The hull was tested and proven against the TM46 anti-tank mine when fitted with a special protection plate under the hull. Additionally, the hull is rated to withstand a 454kg (1,000lb) IED. A mine detonation under a wheel would result in the destruction of the wheel itself but continued operation of the Rooikat. A fire suppression system (automatic &

equipped with a bigger gun necessitated the development of an advanced hydro-pneumatic recoil system which reduced the peak firing force of the main gun. It was slightly longer and weighed 750kg (1,653lb) more which includes the ammunition. The main gun can fire all current NATO types set for the calibre, including APFSDS (see Olifant Mk1A description). Additionally, a 52-calibre thermal sleeve and a larger fume extractor was added. Nine 105mm ready rounds are stored below the turret ring along with the turret basket near the loader station while another seven standby rounds are located in the bustle ammunition rack at the rear of the turret. A further eight rounds are carried in groups of four on either side of the hull. The ergonomic layout allows ten rounds to be fired a minute. The Rooikat 105 retains the hunter-killer, day-night, fire on the move capability of the Rooikat 76. Combined with the high velocity of the round, the Rooikat 105 can defeat the T-72M frontally making it an efficient tank hunter against all MBTs encountered in the region. No orders where ever placed and only one prototype was ever manufactured. The possibility of upgrading some Rooikat 76 with a 105mm gun has surfaced again at the time of writing.

Medium Turret Technology Demonstrator

The MTTD was an independent project to develop and test the feasibility of a 105mm high-pressure and 120mm low-pressure main gun mounted on a remote turret in conjunction with an autoloading system and various other technologies. The loader (left side of the turret) and

Rooikat ZA-35 SPAAG – Public display. (J. Botha)

crew commander (right side of the turret) positions were moved into the hull giving rise to the depressions in the hull on either side of the main gun. The MTTD also features a mock-up of an APS launcher on the rear of the turret. The APS would have increased the survivability of the platform when facing anti-tank missiles. The decision to mount the MTTD on the Rooikat hull was made by the defence industry as it was easier to transport and display. There are no currently known plans for building Rooikats fitted with this turret and gun.

Self-Propelled Air Defence System

During the South African Bush War, the SADF lacked a dedicated modern ground to air defence system which could engage communist/Warsaw Pact-supplied aeroplanes such as the MiG-17, MiG-21, MiG-23 and Mig-25. The skies over Angola were, by the mid-1980s, the most hotly contested airspace in the world. Project Prima (formally known as Project Sterlitzia) was to be South Africa's answer to the desperate need for a modern SPADS which was capable of moving with its mechanised combat groups. The task of designing the SPADS was given to ARMSCOR, Kentron and ESD. Utilising the Rooikat hull with its excellent cross-country mobility was deemed the best option. Two prototypes were completed. One prototype was a SPAAG and the other a SPAAM. Each was fitted with the newly designed EDR 110 radar developed by ESD which could track up to 100 air targets at the same time. The radar antenna was capable of being raised to a height of about 5m (16.4ft) for increased vision which would be very beneficial in the African bush. It was capable of detecting aircraft at 12km (7.45mi) and helicopters at 6km (3.72mi). The entire SPADS system was designed to operate as an integrated air defence system in which targeting data could be shared between nearby SPAAGs\SPAAM and other air defence systems without radars.

Rooikat ZA-35 SPAAG

The Rooikat SPAAG was designated the ZA-35 and would be responsible for close-in air defence. LEW designed a new turret, ammunition feed system and two LEW M-35 35mm guns which were fitted either side of the turret. The guns were capable of firing 1,100 rounds a minute (18.3p/s) of either HE-FRAG against air targets or AP-I against lightly armoured vehicles. The new ammunition feed system was much less complicated and required fewer working parts than other similar systems, thereby easing logistics and reducing the likelihood of breakage. A total of 230+230 rounds were in a ready to fire position and would engage targets in 2-3 second bursts. The computerised FCS featured a fully stabilised electro-optical gunner's sight and tracking system with a high-resolution video camera and a laser rangefinder for optimal target identification and tracking. Additionally, the electro-optical auto tracker allowed passive tracking, which is therefore immune to electronic countermeasures.

Rooikat SPAAM

The Rooikat SPAAM was to provide medium-range air defence utilising the locally developed NGM and SAHV which later became the "*Umkhonto*" (spear) missile. The SPAAM could carry a total of four missiles in pairs on either side of the turret. The SPAAM made use of the same subsystems as the SPAAG which would have eased the required logistic train. With the withdrawal of the SADF from Angola in 1989, the need for such an advanced integrated ground to air defence system was deemed no longer urgently needed. The defence budget saw massive cuts in defence expenditure which ultimately led to the subsequent scrapping of the project.

Combat Vehicle Electric-drive Demonstrator

Following several years of research by ARMSCOR on other platforms, the SANDF approved the fitting of an electric-drive system to a Rooikat. This Rooikat became known as the CVED. Each wheel was fitted with an electric motor measuring 50cm (19.7in). The mechanical drive system was replaced with an electric-drive system which reduced the total weight by 2t. The E-drive system allows the CVED to move short distances without using its diesel engine, which results in a virtually noiseless approach. Although tests proved that an E-drive system could effectively be incorporated into a complex combat system, the project was placed on the

Rooikat SPAAM – Concept model. (P. Victor)

backburner in 2012 due to a lack of funds. There are however plans to potentially upgrade the Rooikat fleet with E-Drive technology in the future.

Rooikat ATGM

The Rooikat ATGM vehicle is a joint offspring of the South African Mechanology Design Bureau and Jordanian King Abdullah II Design and Development Bureau. The purpose was to upgrade the capabilities of the Rooikat to include a direct anti-tank capability. No further information is available.

Rooikat 35/ZT-3

Not much is known about this Rooikat 35. It featured a redesigned turret to accommodate (presumably) a LEW M-35, 35mm gun as well as a ZT3 missile launcher. Only one prototype was built.

OPERATIONAL HISTORY

The Rooikat 76 arrived too late for the South African Bush War. In line with its role in peacekeeping operations, the Rooikat 76 was deployed to conduct internal patrols during South Africa's first democratic election in 1994. In 1998, the country of Lesotho (which is landlocked by South Africa) saw widespread rioting, looting, and lawlessness following a contested election. South Africa, together with Botswana, was tasked by the SADC under Operation Boleas (1998) to restore the rule of law and order in Lesotho. The South African Army deployed the Rooikat 76 from 1SSB to assist the already deployed mechanised units in Lesotho who were engaging in skirmishes with Lesotho army mutineers.

CONCLUSION

The Rooikat armoured car is considered one of the most versatile weapons systems produced by South Africa and in use by the SAAC. Its exceptional mobility, good armament, and balanced protection make the Rooikat 76 one of the most formidable armoured cars in the world, suitable for employment during conventional warfare and peacekeeping operations. According to the defence industry draft document, the Rooikat remains valuable not only in its assigned role but also because it can rapidly deploy in Africa with air transport. Additionally, some Rooikat 76 could in future see an upgrade to 105mm and used for direct combat instead of reconnaissance. The possibility also exists that the diesel-electric drive development will be integrated into the Rooikat and/or South Africa's medium combat vehicle fleet in the future.

A soldier's account with the Rooikat – Mobility!

Watching the Voetspore (a South African 4x4 TV program) crew tackling the sand dunes in the Upington region on SABC 2 this evening in which they start their round South Africa trip in the Northern Cape takes me back to a particularly amusing incident around 1983 during Project Naze which was part of the development of the Rooikat Armoured Car.

We were conducting sand mobility trials at a place some 70km (43.5mi) North of Upington then called Duinestraat, notorious for unforgiving dunes. Present were a number of formidable vehicles such as BTR 60, Cheetah prototypes (proto Rooikat), Unimog plus run of the mill Ratel ICV, Eland armoured car and Land Rovers.

The Potchefstroom University Soil Mechanics (Bodemkundiges) team under the expert guidance of the late Prof Hekkie Harmse had surveyed and selected a particularly steep dune where variables such as tyre selection and pressure, wheel slip, sinkage and suchlike were to be evaluated. Needless to say, the vehicle that got the furthest up the gradient was the BTR 60 with its excellent floatation capabilities.

One day, at around midday, during the course of the evaluation, the members of the evaluation team were gathered at the top of the dune to discuss events of the day. One of the members present pointed to an oncoming dust trail on the road from Upington, which, as it got nearer, could be identified as a VW Kombi. The Kombi could be seen slowing down and, lo and behold, it made a ninety-degree turn to the left and traversed the route to the start point at the very bottom of the specific dune that was marked out as the test dune. The people in the Kombi, who by now had seen our group on the crest of the dune, then proceeded to negotiate the gradient until, barra-biem-barra-boom, it stopped right next to our group and first to dismount was the driver with the announcement, *"Manne, kom ons braai"* (gents let's braai). The Kombi was packed to the brim with a half fuel drum braai wood, utensils, paper plates, fresh meat and of course, as was befitting the occasion, non-alcoholic beverages. Everyone just stood there, dumbfounded with jaws agape until one of the University team members named Johan Broekman asked the driver *"Hoe die donder het jy dit reggekry om hierdie helling te klim?"* (how the hell did you get up this gradient?). The driver answered, *"Krag, momentum en bree bande"* (power, momentum and wide tyres). Need I add, the Kombi had a DJ conversion which, for the non-motoring fraternity means a 3l V6 engine. The vehicle was a Sandock Austral Kombi, and the driver was none other than their big boss, A.J.O. van der Westhuizen (aka Wessie). For the record, urban legend has it that Wessie mastered a four-wheel drift in a Bedford three-tonner.

It took a while for the magnitude of what we had just witnessed to sink in because not one of the multi-million-rand military vehicles could get further than three-quarters of the way up the gradient. In closing, let me just add, the braai was great.

Rooikat CVED – AAD2010. (J. van Zyl)

Lt. Col. (retd) J. French SANDF,
Weapons Systems Officer Tanks

A soldier's account with the Rooikat SPAAG and SPAAM

During the 1980 Angola War, the requirement [for] a Mechanised Anti-Aircraft Guns System, to support the mechanised forces became more and more important. The constant threat of attacks from the air that can cripple a mechanised force in the field unless that defence [is] continuously present and ever alert. This was one of the systems developed beside others. The anticipated air defence system requirements were to keep pace with the tanks, armour[ed] cars and the bulk of the infantry. The design requirements were mobility, fast deployment time with an early warning capability. The 35mm SPAAG would have filled that desperate requirement for close-in air defence.

The project study was completed in 1983 determined that [a] complementary pair of self-contained vehicles each with short range radar for target detection, the one being fitted with 35mm guns (SPAAG) and the other with missiles (SPAAM) for the final target engagements [were required]. These items are fully integrated with their autonomous power supplies in a suitable weapon platform for the SPAAG or SPAAM. The chassis of the South African designed Rooikat armoured car was the chosen weapon platform to ensure mobility and to ease maintenance by using the same common spares as the rest of the mechanised forces on the front line.

It was important that the project must s[t]imulate the local manufacturing market. The project was contracted via Armscor and the private industry in the field of high technology. With the then profitable Kentron as main contractor, supported by Lyttelton Engineering Works and Synertech.

The choice of calibre for the guns was largely dictated by the fact that the South African Army was already using 35mm standard NATO ammunition that was produce[d] by Pretoria Metal Pressing (PMP). This also had the advantage of an extremely high kill probability and of providing the range required to counter attacks from armed helicopters used in the forward line of attack.

LEW were contracted to design and develop a new turret to host the FCS, elect[ro] optic sight, gun system and a crew of two. This turret to fit on the Rooikat [chassis] that was already the preferred vehicle to support the mechanised forces. The computerised FCS featured a fully stabilised electro-optical gunner's sight and tracking system with a high-resolution video camera and a laser rangefinder for optimal target identification and tracking. Additionally, the electro-optical auto tracker allowed passive tracking, which neutralised electronic countermeasures. An FLIR may be fitted to enable targets to be acquired and tracked under conditions of total darkness. The FLIR and rangefinder was developed by Eloptro.

The vehicle commander had a stabilised optical periscope at his disposal to enable him to get a magnified view to the target and assist with identification. The stabilised electro sight and commanders' sight was developed by Kentron

Target detection was done by an acquisition radar mounted at the back of the vehicle with its antenna mounted on a Hydraulic mast. With the antenna in the low operation position the radar had the capability to survey the air space to a hight of 5m (16ft 5in) above ground to a distance of 20km (12.5mi). The radar was developed by SPADS, ESD (South) in Stellenbosch. The state-of-the-art radar had to detect a helicopter even when it was hovering a low altitude amongst heavy ground clutter caused by trees bushes and other ground moving targets.

The whole system was controlled by a ruggedized digital computer system supplied by Synertech. It was powered by an independent diesel operated power supply unit which also supplies cooling air for the operators and equipment.

The SPAAM development was never done beyond a detail paper study. A mock up demonstrator was build. Although the SPAAG and SPAAM have been designed with different capabilities the deployment requirements were to deploy three SPAAG and one SPAAM in a troop organisation formation. Each troop would have been commanded by a troop commander in a Ratel or equivalent vehicle. A fully[sic] battery organisation would have nine SPAAG and three SPAAM with supporting vehicles.

During the early 1990 years, the Project Prima was terminated due to budget constraints. Although the Anti-Aircraft Regiment and South African Mechanised Forces never had the joy of welcomed this most advance air defence system into their arsenal, a huge amount of its building blocks were used on other projects that is still serving the South African Defence Force.

For two consecutive years Project Prima (35mm SPAAG) was awarded the Chairman's Award for the most advanced defence system developed by a completely South African market. The complete absence of imported concepts and sub systems would have made this project a marketing tool on a worldwide basis.

In addition, marking opportunities were explored to the old Eastern block to fit the autonomous turret on a different chassis which included a T-72.

Lt. Col. (retd) A van Heerden, Project Team

12
Mamba Armoured Personnel Carrier

THE AFRICAN MINE TAMING SNAKE
The Mamba APC is one of several South African MPV vehicles which have inspired the modern enclosed V-shaped MRAP vehicles used by Western armies today. The Mamba is still widely used as a vehicle of choice for humanitarian and peacekeeping operations by the UN and is used by several countries for low-intensity conflict operations.

DEVELOPMENT
With the South African Border War still in progress, the rising threat of landmines and IED and civil unrest brewing in the South African townships, the need for an APC was identified. This new vehicle had to be capable of operating in an urban environment while still retaining an anti-mine capability. The goal was to develop an affordable mine-protected APC to be used in a defensive role where needed. The Buffel MPV was well suited for the bush but was too vulnerable in an urban setting due to its open tub (troop compartment). Additionally, the Buffel did not provide its occupants with good protection or situational awareness due to its lack of all-round windows. In the background (1988-1994), a debate was raging in the SADF, especially in the infantry branch, regarding the suitability of various wheeled configurations such as 4x2, 4x4 or 6x6.

The first Mamba 4x2 variant (Mk1) was developed by MECHEM, a subsidiary of the CSIR, which was tasked with the design of concept vehicles for later industrial production. This concept design was done under the leadership of Dr Vernon Joint and his crew within 60 to 90 days. MECHEM reduced much of the limitations of 4x2 vehicles by placing 60% of the vehicle's weight on the drive axle in conjunction with specialised Michelin tyres. This is claimed to nearly equal a 4x4 design in performance.

MECHEM presented two Mamba APCs categorised as Mk1 to the South African Army for trial and evaluation. The Mamba Mk1 made use of Toyota Dyna 5-tonne driveline and parts. The rationale was to

ease logistics as Toyota dealers would have been able to supply parts and services when required making use of off the shelf parts. TFM, an independent company making specialised trucks, was awarded the first industrialisation contract in 1987 for around 157 vehicles. Mobility testing was done at various testing facilities and, once accepted by the SADF, the Mamba was tested at the ARMSCORs Gerotech testing facility in 1987. The mine blast testing was done at the Wallmansthal testing grounds.

Due to a dispute between MECHEM and TFM, MECHEM approached OMC Engineering, a Reunert subsidiary, in 1993 for assistance with vehicle production, which subsequently agreed to do so.

TFM began work on its own 4x4 MPV which was designated RG31. MECHEM found out and immediately set out to produce their own 4x4 version making use of a Buffel Unimog 416-162 drivetrain (left-hand drive) and Mamba Mk1 body. MECHEM once again approached OMC/Sandock Austral, which at the time was being reorganised into Reumech (as Reunert had purchased Sandock Austral), for assistance, and the first prototype was produced in just 28 days and designated Mamba 4x4. The vehicle was taken to Gerotech and shown to the chief of the SADF, who immediately asked how many could be built, to which Sandock Austral responded *"as many Buffels as you have"*. The Mamba 4x4 would, in 1993, cost around R280,000 (R 1,370,000 equivalent

Mamba Mk2 – AAD2018. (D. Venter)

Mamba Mk2 – Driver's compartment. AAD2018. (D. Venter)

Mamba Mk2 – Troop compartment, AAD2018. (D. Venter)

to US$ 94,462 in 2020), which was just a tenth of the cost of the 6x6 APC Sandock Austral had developed at the time. A request for tender was issued in mid-1994, and ultimately Sandock Austral was awarded the contract. Mercedes Exchange Units received the contract from Armscor to strip the Buffel drivetrain (engine, gearbox, axles, drop-down box etc.) to its bare components. These were then evaluated and refurbished where possible to the original manufacturer's specifications in order for Mercedes Benz to be able to supply replacement parts in the future. The drivetrain was delivered to Sandock Austral which was part of the assembly line.

PPM were all right-hand drive, as driving in South Africa is done on the left side, making left-hand drive vehicles illegal to operate on roads as a reduced vision while overtaking other vehicles can be dangerous. An initial five vehicles were produced and taken on a roadshow around various infantry bases around South Africa to test the concept on all terrains and get user feedback. The prototype Mamba was christened "*Modder Varkie*" (Mud Piglet) and, together with several other military vehicles including a Mk1 weapons platform version were sent on a goodwill tour "Peace for Africa" from July to September 1993 with the end destination set at the BMW factory in Europe. The purpose was to test the vehicles in African conditions and promote the vehicles for possible sales. The vehicles performed very well; however, the tour was cut short due to trouble in Central Africa (Burundian Civil War and the Republic of the Congo Civil War).

ARMSCOR drew up a list of requirements according to which the Mamba Mk2 would be tested including small arms fire and mine blast resistance. These mine blast tests were conducted on a PPM at the Wallmansthal testing range, which led to further refinement and improvements in safety that were incorporated into what would become the Mamba Mk2. Around 15 vehicles were produced a month, and the South SANDF took delivery of the Mamba Mk2 in 1994.

During testing, Gerotech found that the Mamba Mk2 engine had difficulty during standardised 60 degree Celsius ambient temperature tests which required redeveloping and was subsequently addressed in the Mk3. The Mk3 prototype was ready in 2002, and mine testing was done in the same year. Additional improvements included improved small arms ballistic protection, improved braking and better stability, improved interior layout, and an overall lower operating cost. In 2006, the contract was awarded for 220 Mamba Mk2 vehicles to be upgraded to Mk3 standard under Project Jury. These vehicles were delivered in two batches of 100 and 120. Between 15 and 20 vehicles were completed a month.

A total of 582 Buffel drivelines would be rebuilt to manufacture the Mamba Mk2. The Mamba Mk2 and Mk3 can be found in all branches of the SANDF and is extensively used by the SA Army. More than 20 countries have purchased Mamba vehicles, with the UN being the lead customer for use in peacekeeping and demining operations globally. Current and former operators include the AU (62), Democratic Republic of the Congo (18), Egypt (14), Equatorial Guinea (25), Estonia (7), Guinea (10), Iraq (115), Ivory Coast (10), Niger (6 – Mk7), Nigeria (25), Sierra Leone (5 – Mk5), South Africa (440), Saudi Arabia (25), South Sudan (10 – Reva-3), Sweden (6), Thailand (207 – Reva 3), Uganda (15), United Arab Emirates (56 – Reva), UN (17), United Kingdom (6 – Alvis 8) and Yemen (112 – Reva 3).

Mamba Mk3 – Stationed in the DRC. Note the roll cage on the roof which also houses a radio antenna. (T. Greyling)

DESIGN FEATURES

The Mamba Mk2 and Mk3 are designed as all-terrain, all-weather MPVs which can operate in urban and rural areas for long-range patrol and transportation of personnel. Mamba's success is due to several key features. It does not have a body, and the frame sits on the wheels at a height of 410mm (16in) off the ground with a V-shaped armoured underbelly which helps disperse and deflect mine blast energy away from the hull, thereby reducing the potential damage. It is of 4×4 design with pneumatically operated differential lock, allowing for effective cross-country use. Making use of commercially available parts reduces its logistical train as spare parts can be supplied easily off the shelf.

Mobility

The Mamba Mk3's 4×4 configuration was designed for the African battlespace and characterised by its versatility and cross-country capability. It has a ground clearance of 316mm (12.4in) and can ford water 1m (3ft 3in) deep and can cross a 0.9m (3ft) wide ditch at a crawl. Its 4x4 configuration allows it to climb a 70% gradient. The Mk2 has a combat weight of 6.8t and the Mk3 6.2t. Both the Mk2 and Mk3 are equipped with the Mercedes Benz OM 352, four-stroke 6-cylinder, water-cooled, direct injection diesel engine which produces 123hp (18.1hp/t for the Mk2 and 19.8hp/t for the Mk3). The engine is located at the front of the vehicle and is coupled to a Mercedes Benz UG 2/30, four-speed manual transmission in the Mk2 and eight-speed synchromesh in the Mk3. The driveline has eight forward (four high and four low) and four reverse gears. It can accelerate from 0-60km/h in 25.2 seconds on a level tar road.

The Mk2 was fitted with drum brakes while the Mk3 was improved by fitting disc brakes. The Mamba Mk2 and Mk3 are claimed to be very stable off-road due to the design of the suspension and powertrain. The Mk2 and Mk3 suspension feature a single coil spring on the front axle and double coil spring on the rear which allows for a high degree of deflecting. The four wheels mount 12:5x20 Michelin XSL all-terrain tyres. Steering is made easier through a hydraulically-assisted recirculating ball system.

Endurance and logistics

The Mamba Mk2 has a 200ℓ (52.8gal) diesel fuel tank which grants it an operational range of 900km (599mi) on road and 450km

(280mi) off-road. The Mk3 has a 160ℓ (42gal) fuel tank which grants it an operational range of 800km (497mi) via road and 400km (249 mi) off-road. They have a maximum road speed of 102km/h (64mph) and can maintain 90km/h on road (56mph) and 25km/h (16mph) cross-country.

Modular design and the commercial nature of the components eases maintenance and reduces the logistical burden. The Mamba is equipped with a B46 internal radio for tactical communications with a 1km range. The Mk2 is fitted with a 100l fresh water tank which can be accessed via a tap above the front left wheel. The Mk3 only has a 50l fresh water tank located on the left rear of the vehicle. The Mamba is equipped with a pneumatic tire inflation system. The system is active when the vehicle is idling with positive air pressure available when the vehicle accelerator is pushed down. The exterior storage bins on both sides of the vehicle are used for vehicle equipment, crew and passenger kits, but are not armoured. The weight of the Mk3 is less than the Mk2 and was achieved by reducing the number and size of the exterior storage bins. The Mamba's light weight makes it easily air transportable via C-130 aeroplane.

Vehicle layout

The Mamba follows a traditional layout with the engine located at the front of the vehicle, driver's compartment in the centre, and troop compartment to the rear. The engine and transmission are protected by the armoured hull to reduce the chances of fatal damage if a mine is detonated.

The Mamba has a crew of two which consists of a driver and commander/gunner. The troop compartment can accommodate nine fully equipped soldiers who are seated facing inward in two rows with five seats on the left and four on the right. Each seat is equipped with a four-point safety harness and a weapon mount for safe storage. The Mk2 has two large rectangular windows on either side of the hull. The Mk3, on the other hand, has smaller side-facing windows. Access to the driver's compartment is through the troop compartment rear door which is opened manually. A hinged step below the door allows for easier access. The driver's compartment has two roof hatches which open to the rear of the vehicle while the troop compartment has six which open to their respective left or right sides of the hull. These hatches can be used as emergency exit points.

Main armament

Although not fitted as standard, several barbette or pintle-mounted weapon systems can be mounted. The weapon system is operated by the commander/gunner through a roof hatch in the driver's compartment. The pintle mount is fitted to the roof, just forward of the commander's hatch. An ammunition rack is located on the roof between the commander's and driver's hatches. Standard weapons include a 7.62mm or 12.7mm BMG and 40mm AGL.

Protection

The Mamba is officially designated a light armoured vehicle by the SANDF. It can protect its occupants against a single TM-57 mine blast under the hull or two TM-57 (12.6kg [27.7lb] TNT equivalent) mine blasts under any wheel. This is achieved by its V-shaped bottom armoured monocoque hull design which deflects blast energy and fragments away from the hull. The fuel tank is externally mounted on the right-hand side of the hull and features a blast-proof cap, thereby reducing the chance that a mine blast would cause a secondary explosion as well as minimising the risk of catastrophic fire to the crew and passengers. The Mk2 and MK3 have a portable fire extinguisher in the driver's compartment.

Mamba Mk3 – Stationed in DRC, note the 12.7mm BMG. (J. Dovey)

The Mk2 hull is rated to protect against 7.62x51mm NATO Ball ammunition. The Mk3 saw an improvement to its ballistic protection level to also include 5.56x45mm NATO Ball ammunition at 30m (98ft) by adding a layer of fibreglass plates. All windows are bulletproof and can protect against multiple small arms fire. The Mk2 and Mk3 driver compartment's left and right window have a firing port each for close-in protection.

The front and rear lights are protected by steel mesh covers. In the centre of the roof to the front, protruding upwards is a wire cutting pole. The purpose is to protect the crew and passengers from wires which can decapitate them while being exposed above the roof hatches.

THE MAMBA FAMILY

Mamba Mk1

The original Mk1 was produced by TFM Industries later (Reumech OMC) and over 500 were built. It was later modified to the Springbuck Mk1, and the Reva Mk1 by ICP. The Puma is yet another variant powered by a Toyota Dyna 7-145 powerplant and drivetrain, quite common in Africa.

Mamba Mk2

The 4×4 built by Sandock Austral for the SADF/SANDF and in service with 18 countries. Additional sub-variants include the Mk2 EE for the Estonian Army, a Mk2 SW for the Swedish Army. The Komanche is a SWB variant of the standard Mk2 and can accommodate seven soldiers. The Sabre had a slightly enlarged driver's compartment which could accommodate four with a rear cargo bay instead of a passenger compartment. The Alvis 4 which is a licence produced version by Alvis UK as well as the Alvis 8, a version of the Komanche SWB.

Mamba Mk3

An up-armoured, ergonomically and technically enhanced version of Mk2. Some 220 SANDF Mk2's were upgraded to Mk3.

Mamba Mk4

N4 Trucks (Pty) Ltd. company has designed and built a new Mamba designated Mk4 in their Pretoria factory. Blast testing by the CSIR showed that the Mk4 can withstand the equivalent blast of 10kg (22lb) TNT under its hull and 14kg (30.9lb) of TNT under any wheel. It is marketed globally by Osprea Logistics and has been deployed by AU peacekeepers in Somalia. Two variants are available, one built on the Magirus air-cooled drive train and the other an Iveco Eurocargo drive train with a water-cooled configuration. In Iraq, it is used by private security contractors.

Mamba Mk5 IVECO and MAGIRUS

The Mk5 IVECO and MAGIRUS are fitted with an Iveco drive train and provides improved ballistic and mine protection, improved performance, mobility and manoeuvrability compared to its predecessors. It retains all of the well-known design and performance capabilities of the Mamba family and is fitted with the latest improvements and modifications required for the new century.

Mamba Mk7 – OSPREA

The latest version of the Mamba by Osprea is the Mk7 which builds on the success of the Mk5 IVECO and Mk5 MAGIRUS. The Mk7 provides even higher degrees of ballistic and mine-blast protection, excellent mobility, and more manoeuvrability than its predecessor. The vehicle is built in the United States of America and has more power, provides innovative tactical capacities, advanced technology, upgraded armour protection, and makes use of US components.

CONCLUSION

The Mamba series of APCs are arguably the trendsetters for the many of the MPVs used today. It has been used by the AU and UN during peacekeeping missions as well as in the Middle East by various countries and military contractors. It is also conceivable that it is the most successful wheeled vehicle design produced to protect armed forces operating in mine-threatened environments in the world. The Mamba range of vehicles have been exported to dozens of countries and saw widespread use in UN, AU peacekeeping missions and peace enforcement operations. It has been widely

Mamba Mk3 – Denel OMC. (B. Naudé)

known for raping, pillaging and murdering civilians and aid workers. The UN Security Council resolution 2098 of 2013 and subsequent resolutions authorised the formation of a FIB in the DRC with peace enforcement mandate. The FIB consists of three infantry battalions, one artillery and one Special Forces and Reconnaissance Company. South Africa makes extensive use of the Mamba for their duties as it excels as a quick reaction APC where the predominant threat is small arms fire and mines.

During late May 2019, a QRF consisting of a platoon (Charlie Company) of 7 SAI on rotation as part of the FIB, responded with four Mamba APCs to an attack on a base at Ngite. While on route they came under attack from ADF rebels who set up trenches. The lieutenant in command ordered the use of 40mm AGL to dislodge the ADF rebels from their trenches. While exiting, the ADF rebels crossed the firing line of the Mamba's mounted 12.7mm BMG. A total of 23 ADF rebels died in the firefight, and a large number of small arms, LMGs and mortars with ammunition were recovered.

copied, and at least five types of derivatives are being sold worldwide under licence.

OPERATIONAL HISTORY

The Mamba is fielded by all South Africa's Motorised Infantry Battalions. As a member of the UN and AU, South Africa is committed to peacekeeping missions in the DRC, Sudan and South Sudan. The eastern part of the DRC, characterised by mountainous terrain, is plagued by rebel factions which are

13
Badger Infantry Combat Vehicle

The Modern African Bushfighter

South Africa has a long tradition of designing highly mobile wheeled armoured vehicles such as the Casspir, Ratel, Rhino and Rooikat. The terrain and climate in the region, as well as the strategic defence needs of South Africa, require a highly mobile ICV able to travel large distances and fulfil a wide variety of roles. The Badger ICV adopts its name from its predecessor, the "Ratel". This animal, despite its small size, is a fierce creature which can sustain a large amount of physical damage as well as inflict it with its long claws. The Badger is therefore well named as its modern armament, enhanced protection, and vastly improved mobility over its predecessor the Ratel make it a formidable opponent. It is designed and produced at a time when South Africa, as a fully-fledged

democracy, is undertaking more peacekeeping responsibilities on the African continent. While its neighbours still rely heavily on Soviet-designed equipment, South Africa chose to continue its tradition of self-reliance by making use of more than 70% local content for the Badger.

Badger – section variant. Mobility course, AAD 2016. (D. Venter)

Project Hoefyster mock-ups at 1 SAI – BAE Land Systems OMC (left), LMT (middle) and Mechanology (right). (D. Venter)

DEVELOPMENT

With the venerable Ratel ICV passing 44 years of service in 2020, the need for a more modern ICV is seen as paramount. Having formed the backbone of South African mechanised battalions for 13 years during the South African Border War and continuing to serve until the present day, the Ratel is starting to show its age. Shortages of dedicated parts make logistics very difficult.

The need for a modern ICV was already laid down in 1995 with the writing of the required operational capability by the SANDF. This was subsequently approved and followed by the staff target and staff requirement, which consists of a functional user requirement and logistical user requirement. In essence, a wish list of capabilities which included the following improvements: troops needed to disembark from the rear of the vehicle, ballistic and mine blast protection, more interior space, firepower and mobility to keep up with MBTs. During the following three years, the SANDF decided to prioritise the modernisation of its Navy and purchased four Valour-class frigates and three 209-class diesel submarines while the Air Force purchased 26 Gripen C/D and 24 Hawk 120 planes.

Badger – section variant, V-incline. (Denel Land Systems)

Badger – section variant, public display, AAD 2018. (D. Venter)

Meanwhile, Project Hoefyster was registered by the SANDF in the late 1990s with the aim of investigating the new requirements. ARMSCOR was tasked with translating these requirements into technical engineering terms. In 2002 the contract was issued by ARMSCOR to four South African companies, IADSA, LMT, MDB and Vickers OMC (later BAE Land Systems OMC and at the time of writing Denel Vehicle Systems). It required a comprehensive development study and a full-sized mock-up of their proposed

Badger – mortar variant, public display, AAD 2018. (D. Venter)

vehicle. ARMSCOR was not completely satisfied with the products and their supporting documentation, and by early 2005, open tenders were sent to 27 companies (local and international), and they were asked to submit proposals and budgets for a new ICV within the timespan of one year. Only one bid was received due to the requirement that the vehicle had to be fitted with the DLS turret. The consortium consisted of the Finnish Patria and its then part-owner, EADS, DLS, OMC and LMT. The proposed vehicle was the Patria's 8x8 AMV, which would be adapted for Southern African battlespace by LMT. Initially, OMC was supposed to manufacture the hulls and DLS the turrets and main armaments. The approved budget for the project was around US$780 million.

In May 2007, DLS was contracted to do the internal fits and supply one prototype of each of the envisaged five variants using the Patria hulls that arrived in South Africa. Each was evaluated and accepted by the SANDF which led to 22 PPM being built by Patria in Finland. During late 2010, the SANDF awarded DLS a further contract to develop additional Badger variants. The then Minister of Defence approved the acquisition plan of Project Hoefyster in Feb 2013 after the initial development phase was complete. The original order called for 264 vehicles but was later reduced to 238. The final number of vehicles to be delivered now rests on 244 ICVs after increasing advance payments to the industry. The final 244 ICVs will consist of 97 section, 14 fire support, 41 mortar, 70 command, 14 missile, and eight ambulance variants. According to Denel, the first battalion of 88 vehicles will be completed by 2022.

The vehicles will be primarily used by 1 SAI Battalion based in Bloemfontein and 8 SAI Battalion based in Upington. Some variants will be allocated for utilisation by brigade headquarters while a small number will be assigned to signal and artillery formations as well as SAMHS and the SAAF. The Badger combines a good mix of firepower, protection and mobility and overshadows all current regional rivals. It is highly manoeuvrable for its size and continues the SANDF's tradition of mobile warfare based on an indirect approach and low force density. The principal tasks of the Badger are variant-specific and include troop transport, fire support, anti-armour, command and control, and medical transport.

DESIGN FEATURES
The design, development and production of the Badger were undertaken due to the need for a more modern ICV to replace the Ratel presently in service with the SANDF. The Badger is characterised by eight big wheels, mobility, bush breaking ability, and versatility as a weapons platform which will be well adapted for its role as a modern ICV in the Southern African battlespace.

Mobility
The African battlespace favours a wheeled configuration, which makes the Badger the perfect candidate for its role as an ICV. The Badger makes use of an automatic ZF gearbox with seven forward and one reverse gear with the option for the driver to also change gears manually if required. The Badger can ford 1.2m (3.9ft) of water without preparation and has 400mm (15.8in) of ground clearance. It is powered by a Scania fuel-injected diesel engine which produces 543hp (405kW) at 2100rpm and provides 20hp/t. This horsepower to weight ratio allows the Badger to accelerate from 0-60km/h (0-37mph) in under 20 seconds and 60-100km/h (37-62mph) in under 40 seconds and achieve a top speed of 104km/h (64mph). The Badger retains 70% mobility with the loss of one wheel and 30% with the loss of two wheels. The wheels feature a central tire inflation system. It can cross a 2m (6ft 7in) trench at a 3km/h (1.9mph) crawl, and can climb a gradient of 60%, and has a side slope rating of 30%. The suspension system makes use of hydro-pneumatic struts which allows for true independent wheel movement over rough terrain, thereby dramatically increasing the stability of the vehicle and ensuring a smoother ride for the occupants. All wheels are equipped with ABS brakes. The APU allows all on-board systems to remain powered even if the engine is switched off.

Endurance and logistics
The fuel capacity of the Badger is 450ℓ (119gal) which allows it to travel 1,000km (621mi) on the road and 500km (311mi) off-road. A 190ℓ (50gal) is stored in the left fuel tank and 230ℓ (61gal) in the right one, while another 27ℓ (7gal) is located in the transfer tank. The Badger is fitted with a mix of up to two VHF, three HF tactical radios which allow for reliable inter-crew and multivehicle communication. This command and control system enhances the ICV's force multiplier effect on the battlefield. The Badger features four built-in drinking water tanks with a total capacity of 130ℓ (34gal).

Vehicle layout
Most Badgers carry a standard complement of four crew members, consisting of the section commander, vehicle commander, gunner, and driver. The section commander is responsible for leading his section when disembarking from the Badger while the vehicle commander is responsible for commanding the vehicle. The vehicle commander station is located on the left side and the gunner's station on the right of the turret. The section commander is positioned behind the driver who is seated in the forward left side of the hull. Each station in the turret has six vision blocks which provide a 270-degree field of view. The vehicle commander has at his disposal a day video sight which offers a stabilised 360-degree capability. Both

The vehicle commander and the gunner have a 360-degree situational awareness through episcopes and multi-function flat-panel video displays. Additionally, the vehicle commander has the ability, via the video sight, to override the gunner's control and slave the main gun onto a target. The gunner's station is fitted with an x8 day and night, thermal sight periscope as well as an auxiliary gunner sight with direct view optics with aiming reticules. Entry and exit for the former and latter are through the gunner's and vehicle commander's cupola. In an emergency, the gunner and vehicle commander can escape through the rear of the vehicle. The driver's station is located on the front left of the hull and is accessible through the fighting compartment or a single-piece hatch above the driver's station. The driver's station is adjustable and features three periscopes for enhanced vision and situational awareness. The central periscope can be substituted with a passive night driving periscope allowing full day/night capability. The driver can make use of compressed air to clean his periscopes while closed down, a feature particularly useful in the dusty climates in which the Badger will operate. The driver makes use of a power-assisted steering wheel to drive while acceleration and braking are controlled with foot pedals.

The rear compartment has seating space for passengers – the number of which is variant-specific. The Badger's crew and passenger compartment feature an air conditioning unit, which helps reduce crew and passenger fatigue. The passenger seats face inward and are fitted to a frame which is attached to the hull in such a way that should a mine detonate under a wheel or under the hull the minimum amount of mine blast energy reaches the passenger seats, thereby reducing the possibility of spinal injury. Additionally, each seat is fitted with a footrest which allows the passenger across from the seat to rest their feet off the floor, also to reduce the possibility of injury should a mine be detonated. The Badger is fitted with several hull encased, all-round camera video system for enhanced situational awareness. The troop compartment is equipped with several monitors displaying the camera views and a dedicated section leader monitor for planning and presentation purposes. The hydraulically operated rear door was designed in South Africa and doubles as a weapons and equipment rack which can hold entrenching tools, LMGs, 40mm six-round grenade launchers, RPG-7s, 60mm patrol mortars and ammunition for the aforementioned weapons. The advantage of such an arrangement is that it frees up the troop compartment from unnecessary clutter and

Badger – ambulance variant. (Denel Land Systems)

provides quick access to troops disembarking from the rear. Entry and exit from the rear door is made more accessible by a step which deploys mechanically as the door opens and retracts when the rear door closes.

Main armament

The Badger makes use of the LCT which forms part of a MICT family developed by Denel as part of the NGICV programme for the SANDF. The turret family is built around the FMC principle, which allows various weapons and sighting systems to be integrated with ease. Such a design reduces logistic requirements, operational costs, training time, and ensures maximum commonality and re-use of components within the modules. Both the section variant and the fire support variant make use of the LCT-30 turret which can make a full 360-degree rotation in 13 seconds. The mortar variant is equipped with the LCT-60 while the command variant is equipped with the LCT-12.7, and the missile variant uses the LCT-Missile turret. The section variant is armed with a Denel 30mm dual-feed linkless Camgun (EMAK 30) which can engage targets effectively at 4km (2.48mi). The Camgun features a double battle muzzle brake and has a single recoil mechanism. The rapid-fire consists of a three round burst mode which provides 60 rounds per minute. Empty cartridges are ejected on the left side of the turret. The section variant carries 400x30mm cannon rounds. The rounds carried consist of APFSDS for use against armoured targets and

Badger – missile variant. (Denel Land Systems)

Badger – missile variant, Wallmannsthal testing grounds. (R. du Plessis)

SAPHEI for use against soft targets. Literature searches reveal that modern 30mm cannon rounds such as the APFSDS have a muzzle velocity of 1,430m/s and can penetrate up to 100mm of RHA at zero degrees at 1km (0.6mi). This is significant considering that IFV such as the BMP-2 and BMP-3 only have 33mm (1.29in) and 35mm (1.37in) of frontal armour respectively. Furthermore, this means that the Badger section variant is capable of knocking out T-54/55, T-62 and T-72M MBT found in the region from the sides and rear from range. It should, however, be stressed that the section variant is not supposed to engage MBTs directly. The SAPHEI has a muzzle velocity of 1,100m/s (3601 ft/s) and can penetrate 30mm (1.18in) of RHA at 30 degrees at 200m (219 yards).

All but the ambulance variant are armed with a co-axial 7.62mm BMG with a total of 4,000 rounds which consists of 20 belts of 200 rounds each. The vehicle commander has at his disposal a stabilised panoramic sight and a primary stabilised main sight which can track targets automatically. All variants have a day/night sight capability as standard with some variation of the fire-control system which is variant-specific.

Fire control system

The Badger is equipped with the FDS digital FCS which receives information from a laser rangefinder and accurately places rounds on target with the main gun. The laser rangefinder is accurate to within 5m x 5m (16.4ft x 16.4ft) at 10km (6.2mi). The variations are automatically calculated and compensated for according to the ammunition selected by the gunner. The FCS allows the gunner to select a target in less than two seconds. The fire solution is given, allowing the gunner to fire on target which adjusts the main gun auto-lay aim. The commander can override the gunner's aim with the flip of a switch to put the main gun on target. This effectively provides the Badger with hunter-killer capability. The digital FCS allows hits on a moving target while the Badger is on the move itself by adjusting the main gun's aim after taking into account the distance to the target, the relative speeds and relative direction, thereby maximising the single-shot hit probability. The single-shot hit probability while static at a 2.4m x 2.4m (7.9ft x 7.9ft) target at 2km (1.24mi) is greater than 65%.

Protection

The Badger is based on the Finnish Patria AMV. Unlike its European counterpart, the Badger has numerous modifications such as dedicated bush protection to enhance its durability for use in the African bush. The Badger features a dual hull design to enhance survivability against kinetic and HEAT projectiles. The total thickness of the outer/inner hull and add-on armour package and composition thereof are classified. The outer hull (which can be removed) functions as a first-line defence against light and medium arms. This is followed by an empty space of classified width which can act either as spaced armour or can be fitted with an add-on armour package developed by ARMSCOR Armour Technology Institute. The add-on armour over the frontal arc is left in place during peacetime whereas the left and right sides add-on armour is removed. Lastly is the inner hull which serves as the last line of defence. The inner hull is fitted with an anti-spall lining to reduce crew vulnerability to fragments in case of penetration. It was reported from Afghanistan, where the Badger's cousin the Patria was deployed, that two such vehicles equipped with add-on armour package, survived direct hits from RPG-7s which did not penetrate the inner hull. It is unclear what types the RPG rounds were involved. The Badger is protected against 30mm APFSDS rounds over the frontal arc and 23mm AP rounds around the remaining hull. The roof is rated against heavy artillery blast and fragmentation.

Due to the prevalence of anti-tank and anti-personnel landmines in Sub-Saharan Africa, the Badger features a flat bottom mine-protected hull (not found in the Patria) which absorbs the blast and shock produced by a mine detonation. The technology was developed by LMT and offers protection against the equivalent of a 6kg (13lb) mine anywhere under the hull.

The Badger features two automatic fire suppression systems, one for the engine and the other for the crew/troop compartment. The system can also be engaged manually. The Badger is fully NBC capable as it comes standard with an overpressure system. Two banks of two smoke grenade launchers are located on the roof of the turret, behind the commander's and gunner's station to protect them from damage when bundu bashing. The hull headlamps are encased in the hull, and an armoured screen was added to protect them from damage while bundu bashing. A recent addition to al

Badger – missile variant, Wallmansthal testing grounds. (R. du Plessis)

the Badger variants is a guide rail/cage on the turret, the primary purpose of which is to guide branches over the commander's sight to avoid damage to it.

THE BADGER FAMILY

Currently, there are six variants of the Badger, of which five are armed, namely the section variant (30 mm), fire support variant (30mm), mortar variant (60mm), command variant (12.7mm) and missile variant (Ingwe). The ambulance variant is not armed.

Section variant

The section variant is armed with a Denel 30mm dual-feed linkless Cam Gun (EMAK 30) which can engage targets up to 4km when firing one round at a time. Rapid-fire consists of 3-round bursts. The section variant carries 400, 30x173mm rounds. The rear compartment of the section variant has seating space for four passengers on the left and three passengers on the right.

Fire support variant

The fire support variant carries the same main armament as the section variant but has additional main armament ammunition which is kept in storage racks on the right-hand side of the passenger compartment. Seating in the passenger compartment is limited to two for use by a dedicated two-man anti-tank team.

Mortar variant

The primary purpose of the mortar variant is to supply indirect fire support to attacking forces. It is equipped with a 60mm DLS breech-loading, water-cooled mortar which can engage targets directly at 1.5km (0.9mi) in line of sight or 6.2km (3.9mi) indirectly. The mortar variant carries 256 60mm bombs and has a firing rate of six bombs per minute and accuracy of 2.4m x 2.4m (7.9 ft x 7.9ft) at 1.5km (0.93mi). It has a 40% better lethality and effectiveness than the old 81mm mortar bombs. The variant has four crew members, namely the vehicle commander, gunner, driver, and technician. The bombs are kept in bin racks on either side of the rear compartment with the technician's seat on the left.

Command variant

The command variant is armed with a primary 12.7mm BMG which allows more room for C&C equipment and personnel. The command variant carries 1,200 x 12.7mm rounds. This variant has a standard crew of three (driver, vehicle commander, and gunner) and two to three communication staff in the rear.

Missile variant

The missile variant is armed with the Denel Dynamics "Ingwe" (Leopard) ZT3A2 laser-guided, jam-resistant, a beam-riding missile which has an effective engagement range of over 5km (3.1mi). The Ingwe has a tandem warhead that can defeat ERA and can penetrate up to 1,000mm (39.4in) of RHA at zero degrees. On either side of the turret is a missile launcher system, which accommodates two missiles. When not in use, the missile launcher reverts to a 45-degree nose down sloped position behind a protective plate to protect the launcher from small arms fire and possible damage when bundu bashing. When a target is to be engaged, the missile launcher's nose rises 45 degrees up to a level position, from where the missile can be fired. A total of 12 missiles is carried in the rear compartment racks on either side of the hull. The missile variant carries a driver, vehicle commander, gunner and loader. The missile launchers are rearmed from within the vehicle via guide rails. The missile variant launcher is backwards compatible with the Swift missile. Each ZT-3B weighs 34kg (75lb) and requires two people to load.

Ambulance variant

The ambulance variant has a crew complement of three which consists of a driver and two medical personnel. The ambulance variant has no turret and instead has a higher roof than the other variants. It features an effective patient handling system allowing for the minimum effort of moving patients using rails and a winch system. The rear compartment is better lit than the other variants. Three patients lying down can be carried at a time or two patients lying down and four seated.

CONCLUSION

The Badger is the first new ICV in the SANDF inventory since the Ratel was introduced in 1975. The Badger is one of the best-protected vehicles of its class in the world. This, combined with its mobility and firepower, makes for a formidable adversary. As such, the Badger is a worthy successor and vast improvement over its predecessor, the Ratel. Although the cost of the Badger might seem high to most, it is very affordable when compared to other modern wheeled ICVs such as the MOWAG Piranha, Boxer and French IFV.

Bibliography

61 Mech Battalion Group Veterans Association. 2016. Olifant Mk1A. http://www.61mech.org.za/equipment/olifant-mk-1a Accessed: 16\09\17

61 Mech Battalion Group Veterans Association. 2019. Ratel 12.7. http://www.61mech.org.za/equipment/ratel-127-command Accessed: 02\12\19

61 Mech Battalion Group Veterans Association. 2019. Ratel 20. http://www.61mech.org.za/equipment/ratel-20 Accessed: 02\12\19

61 Mech Battalion Group Veterans Association. 2019. Ratel 60. http://www.61mech.org.za/equipment/ratel-60 Accessed: 02\12\19

61 Mech Battalion Group Veterans Association. 2019. Ratel 81. http://www.61mech.org.za/equipment/ratel-81 Accessed: 02\12\19

61 Mech Battalion Group Veterans Association. 2019. Ratel 90. http://www.61mech.org.za/equipment/ratel-90 Accessed: 02\12\19

61 Mech Battalion Group Veterans Association. 2019. Ratel ZT-3. http://www.61mech.org.za/equipment/ratel-zt-3 Accessed 02\12\19

Abbot, P., Heitman, H.R. & Hannon, P., *Modern African Wars (3): South-West Africa.* (Oxford: Osprey Publishing, 1991)

Armed Forces. 1991. Magazine. November edition.

ARMY-GUIDE.COM. 2012. The G6 -Still outgunning the competition. http://army-guide.com/eng/article/article_2406.html#.T2JSURBZGMs. Accessed: 12\04\17

ARMY-GUIDE.COM. 2017. Casspir MK III. Accessed: 09\07\17

ARMY-GUIDE.COM. 2019. Buffel. http://www.army-guide.com/eng/product1080.html Accessed: 20\09\17.

Baxter, P. 2015. Casspir appreciation group. Groundshout post: 6 Dec. 2015. Accessed: 27\08\17

Beyleveldt, J. 2017. SA Pantserskool – SA Army School of Armour (SAW/SANW). Facebook post. Accessed: 16\09\17

Botha, W.C., de Vries, R., Ehlert, J, Haddad, W., Nell, J.T., Savides, T. & van der Westhuizen, A.J.O., *Ratel: The making of a Legend. Volume 2: Life with Ratel.* (Pretoria: BusinessPrint, 2020)

Bouwer, M. 2019. Buffel operation doctrine. Facebook correspondence GRENSOORLOG/ BORDER WAR 1966-1989. Accessed: 20\09\19

Camp, S. & Heitman, H.R., *Surviving the ride: A pictorial history of South African manufactured mine protected vehicles* (Pinetown: 30° South Publishers. 2014)

Citizen Reporter. 1993/4. The Citizen: SA tank 'compares with the best in the world'. Date of publication: unknown.

Collins, D.C. 2017. SA Pantserskool – SA Army School of Armour (SAW/SANW). Facebook post. https://web.facebook.com/groups/2609116067/search/?query=dewald%20Collins&epa=SEARCH_BOX Accessed: 16\09\17

Combat and Survival. 1991. Bush fighting with the Ratel: Volume 12. Westport, Connecticut: H.S. Stuttman Inc.

Combat and Survival. 1991. On externals with the Eland. Volume 23. Westport, Connecticut: H.S. Stuttman Inc.

de Vries, R., *Eye of the Firestorm: Strength lies in mobility* (Tyger Valley: Naledi, 2013)

de Vries, R., Burger, C. & Steenkamp, W. *Mobile Warfare for Africa: On the Successful Conduct of Wars in Africa and Beyond – Lessons Learned from the South African Border War* (Solihul: Helion and Company, 2018)

DEFENCEWEB. 2009. SANDF projects: past, present & future. https://www.defenceweb.co.za/sa-defence/sa-defence-sa-defence/sandf-projects-past-present-future/ Accessed: 20/01/19

DEFENCEWEB. 2011. Army cares for Casspir. https://www.defenceweb.co.za/land/land-land/army-cares-for-casspir/ Accessed: 29/06/20.

DEFENCEWEB. 2011. Fact file: Denel FV2 Bateleur Multiple Launch Rocket System (MLRS). https://www.defenceweb.co.za/resources/fact-files/fact-file-denel-fv2-bateleur-multiple-launch-rocket-system-mlrs/?catid=79%3Afact-files&Itemid=159 Accessed: 13/12/19

DEFENCEWEB. 2011. Fact file: G6 L45 self-propelled towed gun-howitzer. http://www.defenceweb.co.za/index.php?option=com_content&view=article&id=13537:fact-file-g6-l45-self-propelled-towed-gun-howitzer-&catid=79:fact-files&Itemid=159 Accessed: 18/04/17

DEFENCEWEB. 2011. R96.8m for Olifant, Rooikat ammo. http://www.defenceweb.co.za/index.php?option=com_content&view=article&id=18165:r968m-for-olifant-rooikat-ammo&catid=50:Land&Itemid=105 Accessed: 30/11/18

DEFENCEWEB. 2013. South African National Defence Force. Available at http://www.defenceweb.co.za/index.php?option=com_content&view=article&id=29273:south-africa&catid=119:african-militaries&Itemid=255 Accessed: 30/11/18

DEFENCEWEB. 2016. SANDF projects. https://www.defenceweb.co.za/sa-defence/sa-defence-sa-defence/sandf-projects/ Accessed: 10/06/17

DEFENCEWEB. 2017. First locally produced pre-production Badger expected later this year. https://www.defenceweb.co.za/sa-defence/sa-defence-sa-defence/first-locally-produced-pre-production-badger-expected-later-this-year/?catid=111%3Asa-defence&Itemid=242 Accessed: 05/05/18

DEFENCEWEB. 2019. Rheinmetall resets the range goal posts. https://www.defenceweb.co.za/featured/rheinmetall-resets-the-range-goal-posts/ Accessed: 20/11/19

DEFENCEWEB. 2019. Mamba could be used by SAMHS as a combat ambulance. https://www.defenceweb.co.za/featured/mamba-could-be-used-by-samhs-as-a-combat-ambulance/ Accessed: 15/12/19

DEFENCEWEB. 2019. South African soldiers repulse ADF rebels in DRC firefight. https://www.defenceweb.co.za/featured/south-african-soldiers-repulse-adf-rebels-in-drc-firefight/ Accessed: 16/12/19

DEFENCEWEB. 2020 Denel outlines its main South African projects and programmes. https://www.defenceweb.co.za/industry/industry-industry/denel-outlines-its-main-south-african-projects-and-programmes/?fbclid=IwAR2fPwWIq8XlwzZjAlVz2culTn55cpzZYD-GS50CY5qNKF30osvjvsuWjnY Accessed: 29/07/20

DENEL. Date unknown. Armoured Sighting System: CS60 – Primary Stabilized Gunner Sight. http://sturgeonshouse.ipbhost.com/topic/652-general-afv-thread/page/90/Accessed: 20/02/19

DENEL. Date unknown. Gunner Armoured Sighting System: GS60 – Primary Stabilized Gunner Sight. http://sturgeonshouse.ipbhost.com/topic/652-general-afv-thread/page/90/ Accessed: 20/02/19

DENEL. 2007. Rooikat 105 Armoured Fighting Vehicle. http://admin.denel.co.za/uploads/rooikat_76.pdf Accessed: 23/11/19

DENEL. 2012. The G6 – still outgunning the competition after 25 years. http://admin.denel.co.za/uploads/41_Denel_Insights.pdf Accessed: 25/04/17

DENEL. 2018. Advanced modular infantry combat turret. http://admin.denel.co.za/uploads/AMICT.pdf Accessed: 22/04/18.

DENEL. 2018. Media center. http://www.denel.co.za/album/Armour-Products/41 Accessed. 09/01/18

Foss, C.F. 1989. Rooikat: ARMSCOR's new hit-and-run lynx. International Defense Review, 22 (November):1563-1566.

Foss, C.F. 2004. *Jane's Armour and Artillery. Volume 25*. (Coulsden: Jane's Information Group Ltd, 2004)

Gardner, D. 2020. Former Director OMC Engineering. Olifant improvements. South African Defence Industry & Military Related. Facebook post. https://web.facebook.com/groups/79284870944/ 02/04/20

Gardner, D. 2019. Former Director OMC Engineering. Eland hull and turret development. Private Facebook correspondence. 12/06/19

Gardner, D. 2017. Former Director OMC Engineering. SA Pantserskool – SA Army School of Armour (SAW/SANW). Facebook post. https://web.facebook.com/groups/2609116067/ Accessed: 30/09/17

GLOBAL SECURITY.ORG. 2015. Olifant Mk1B. https://www.globalsecurity.org/military/world/rsa/olifant-1b.htm Accessed: 16/09/17

GLOBAL SECURITY.ORG. 2016. Hoefyster (Horseshoe) / Badger. https://www.globalsecurity.org/military/world/rsa/badger.htm Accessed: 04/05/18.

GLOBAL SECURITY.ORG. 2017. Wheel versus Track. Accessed: http://www.globalsecurity.org/military/systems/ground/wheel-vs-track.htm 12/04/17

Harmse, K. & Sunstan, S., *South African Armour of the Border War 1975-89*. (Oxford: Osprey Publishing, 2017)

Heitman, H.R. *Krygstuig van Suid-Afrika*. (Struik, 1988)

Heyneke, D. 2018. Bateleur FV2 project team member and instructor on the Visarend. Private Facebook correspondence. Accssed: 16/11/18

Jordan, L. 2017. Tankers in Angola. Facebook post. https://web.facebook.com/groups/435796636442928/ Accessed: 16/09/17

Jordan, L. 2017. Tankers in Angola. Facebook post. https://web.facebook.com/groups/435796636442928/ Accessed: 30/09/17

Joubert, K. 2019. Former ARMSCOR Senior Manager in the Acquisition Department. Buffels history and technical details. Email correspondence. 02/11/19

Joubert, K. 2019. Former ARMSCOR Senior Manager in the Acquisition Department. Number of Buffels sold internationally. Telephone interview. 23/10/19

LITNET. 2013. "Krag lê in mobiliteit" – Roland de Vries gesels oor Eye of the Firestorm. https://www.litnet.co.za/krag-l-in-mobiliteit-roland-de-vries-gesels-oor-eye-of-the-firestorm/ Accessed: 18/11/16

Martin, G. 2016. Defence Equipment for South Africa. Military Technology, 40(9): 64-69.

Melinda, P. 2019. Media Statement – Denel Artillery Reaches New Milestone. http://www.denel.co.za/press-article/Denel-Artillery-Reaches-New-Milestone/224 Date: 12/11/19

MILITARY FACTORY. 2017. Denel GV6 Renoster (G6 Rhino) 6×6 Wheeled Self-Propelled Artillery (SPA). http://www.militaryfactory.com/armor/detail.asp?armor_id=436 Accessed: 08/04/17

Moukambi, V. *Relations between South Africa and France with special reference to military matters, 1960-1990* (Stellenbosch: Stellenbosch University, 2008)

Naish, H. 2017. Tankers in Angola. Facebook post. https://web.facebook.com/groups/435796636442928/ Accessed: 30/09/17

NAMMO. 2018. Nammo ammunition handbook. 5th Ed. https://www.nammo.com/globalassets/pdfs/ammobook/nammo_ammo_handbook_aw_screen.pdf Accessed: 15/04/18

NATIONAL DEFENCE INDUSTRY COUNCIL. 2017. Defence industry strategy: version 5.8, draft. http://www.dod.mil.za/advert/ndic/doc/Defence%20Industry%20Strategy%20Draft_v5.8_Internet.pdf Accessed. 11/01/18

Nell, S. 2020. Badger development. Founder of LMT and CEO of ADGM. Email correspondence. 16/02/20

Niemann, P. 2017. SA Pantserskool – SA Army School of Armour (SAW/SANW). Facebook post. Accessed: 16/09/17

Oosthuizen, G.J.J. 2004. Regiment Mooirivier and South African transborder operations into Angola during 1975/76 and 1983/4. Historia, 49(1): 135-153.

OPSREA. 2019. Mamba Mk7. http://osprea.com/vehicles/armoured/mamba-mk7/ Accessed: 13/12/19

OPSREA. 2019. Mamba Mk5 Iveco. Accessed: 13/12/19

ORDNANCE & MUNITIONS FORECAST. 2015. G6 Renoster 155mm Self-Propelled Howitzer. https://www.forecastinternational.com/archive/disp_pdf.cfm?DACH_RECNO=1105 Accessed: 08/04/17

REUMECH-OMC. Date unknown. TTD technical specification brochure. http://sturgeonshouse.ipbhost.com/profile/1197-stimpy75/content/page/6/?type=forums_topic_post Accessed: 12/09/18

Reynolds, J. 2012. Denel Land Systems Shows GI-30: 30mm Camgun. *African Armed Forces Journal*, 2:11.

RVF. 2019. Armored Vehicle Market Report 2019. Mamba numbers. http://rfventures.co/wp-content/uploads/2019/02/Armored-vehicles-market-2019.pdf Accessed: 15/12/19

SA ARMY. 2010. Vehicles: Mamba. http://www.army.mil.za/equipment/vehicles/mamba.htm Accessed: 07/12/19

SA ARMY. 2010. Weapon systems infantry: Grenade Launchers. http://www.army.mil.za/equipment/weaponsystems/infantry/Y2_Y3_Grenade_Launchers.htm Accessed: 07/12/19

SA ARMY. 2010. Weapon systems infantry: Machine Guns. http://www.army.mil.za/equipment/weaponsystems/infantry/Machine_Guns.htm Accessed: 07/12/19

Sabatier, P. 2015. This is not a front for something...it's a Casspir appreciation group. Groundshout post: 6 Dec. 2015. https://web.facebook.com/groups/19835125223/ Accessed: 27/09/17

Sabatier, P. 2019. This is not a front for something...it's a Casspir appreciation group. Groundshout post: 11 Jun. 2019. https://web.facebook.com/groups/19835125223/ Accessed: 11/06/19

Sabatier, P. 2020. Olifant Mk1A. Email correspondence: 01/0420

SALUT Magazine. 1996. Advance technology. October Edition.

SANDF personnel. 2017. Interview and vehicle inspection G6-45. School of Artillery Klipdrift Military Base, Potchefstroom.

SANDF personnel. 2017. Interview and vehicle inspection, Bateleur FV2. School of Artillery Klipdrift Military Base, Potchefstroom.

SANDF personnel. 2018. Interview and vehicle inspection Bateleur FV2. African Aerospace and Defence 2018, Waterkloof Air Force Base, Pretoria.

SA-SOLDIER.COM. 2019. Buffel. https://www.sa-soldier.com/data/07-SADF-equipment/ Accessed: 20/09/19

Savides A. 2016. Brig Gen (retd) – Ratel development, history and application. Private Facebook correspondence. Accessed: 05/11/16

Savides A. 2019. Brig Gen (retd) – 61 Base Workshop. Private Facebook correspondence. Accessed: 04/10/19

Savides A. 2019. Brig Gen (retd) – Eland hull and turret development. Facebook correspondence on Pantserbond/Armour Association. https://web.facebook.com/groups/pantserbond/ Accessed: 12/06/19

Savides A. 2019. Brig Gen (retd) – Buffel MPV. Email correspondence. 30/09/19.

Schenk, R. 2019. SSgt (retd) – Eland turret rear tube uses. Facebook correspondence on Pantserbond/Armour Association. https://web.facebook.com/groups/pantserbond/ Accessed: 12/06/19

Selfe, A. 2019. Eland lights. Facebook correspondence on Pantserbond/Armour Association. Accessed: 12/06/19

Steenkamp, W. & Heitman, H.R. *Mobility Conquers: The Story of 61 Mechanised Battalion Group 1978-2005* (Solihull: Helion & Company Limited, 2016)

Stiff, P. *Taming the Landmine* (Alberton, South Africa: Galago Publishing, 1986)

Swanepoel, D. 2019. Buffel operation doctrine. Facebook correspondence GRENSOORLOG/ BORDER WAR 1966-1989. https://web.facebook.com/groups/324092157716653/ Accessed: 20/09/19

Van der Linde, S. 2019. Buffel operation doctrine. Facebook correspondence GRENSOORLOG/ BORDER WAR 1966-1989. https://web.facebook.com/groups/324092157716653/ Date 20/09/19

Van der Merwe, C. 2019. First 19 Buffels. Facebook correspondence GRENSOORLOG/ BORDER WAR 1966-1989. https://web.facebook.com/groups/324092157716653/ Accessed 04/10/19

Van der Waag, I. *A military history of modern South Africa* (Jeppestown: Jonathan Ball Publishers, 2015)

Van Wyngaard. 2020. Olifant Mk1B acceleration. Facebook correspondence SA Pantserskool – SA School of Armour (SAW/SANW). https://web.facebook.com/groups/2609116067/10158003967556068/?comment_id=10158003985236068&reply_comment_id=10158004433316068&notif_id=1589560322956998&notif_t=group_comment Accessed: 04/04/20

VEG Magazine. 2005. The development of the Olifant tank: Centurion Mk3. Issue 2. Victor Logistics.

VEG Magazine. 2005. The development of the Olifant tank: Centurion Mk5. Issue 3. Victor Logistics.

VEG Magazine. 2005. The development of the Olifant tank: Goodbye to the Centurion. Issue 4. Victor Logistics.

VEG Magazine. 2005. The development of the Olifant tank: Olifant Mk1A & 1A GHV. Issue 7. Victor Logistics.

VEG Magazine. 2005. The development of the Olifant tank: Olifant Mk1A. Issue 6. Victor Logistics.

VEG Magazine. 2005. Die vervanging van 'n legende: Projek Hoefyster. Issue 8. Victor Logistics.

VEG Magazine. 2005. The development of the Olifant Mk1B & Mk2. Issue 8. Victor Logistics.

Viljoen, C.R. 2019. Eland 60 driver. Interview. 09/06/19

Volker, W. 1994. PARATUS: LEW smooth-bore gun for the Tank Technology Demonstrator. Feb, page 67.

Voortrekker Monument Military Festival. 2018. SANDF information display: Olifant Mk2 Main Battle Tank.

WAR IN ANGOLA. 2017. Vehicle specifications, 4:14. http://www.warinangola.com:8088/Default.aspx?tabid=1051 Accessed: 08/04/17

WASHINGTON POST. 1988. S. Africa unveils war machine for sale abroad. https://www.washingtonpost.com/archive/politics/1988/10/23/s-africa-unveils-war-machine-for-sale-abroad/47974c0b-101b-4d9b-9e54-c303061f3db2/?utm_term=.4128664bf15d Accessed. 11/01/18

Widd, P. 2019. Buffel operation doctrine. Facebook correspondence GRENSOORLOG/ BORDER WAR 1966-1989. Date 20/09/19.

WORLD HERITAGE ENCYCLOPEDIA. 2019. Mamba APC. http://self.gutenberg.org/articles/Mamba_APC Accessed: 07/12/19

Zulkamen, I. 1994. From the 'Red Kestrel' to the 'Red Cat' – South Africa's Rooikat 105 AFV. *Asian Defence Journal*, 4 (1994): 42.

INTERVIEWS
Eland

Ansley, L. 2019. Eland 20 armoured car. Private Facebook correspondence on Pantserbond/Armour Association. 30/06/19

Bowden, N. 2019. Cpt SANDF. Eland armoured car. Private Facebook correspondence on Pantserbond/Armour Association. 12/06/19

Gardner, D. 2019. Former Director OMC Engineering. Eland hull and turret development. Private Facebook correspondence on Pantserbond/Armour Association. 12/06/19

Marais, S. 2019. Curator SA Armour Museum. Eland armoured car. Telephone correspondence. 14/06/19

Savides A. 2019. Brig Gen (retd). Eland hull and turret development. Facebook correspondence on Pantserbond/Armour Association. 12/06/19

Schenk, R. 2019. SSgt (retd). Eland turret rear tube uses. Facebook correspondence on Pantserbond/Armour Association. 12/06/19

Selfe, A. 2019. Eland lights. Facebook correspondence on Pantserbond/Armour Association. 12/06/19

Buffel

Barnard, C. 2019. 61 Base Workshop, Buffel production. Facebook correspondence GRENSOORLOG/ BORDER WAR 1966-1989. 20/10/19

Beyl, M. 2019. Operation Sceptic 1980. Facebook correspondence SMOKESHELL. 10 JUNE 1980. 22/10/19

Bouwer, M. 2019. Buffel operation doctrine. Facebook correspondence GRENSOORLOG/ BORDER WAR 1966-1989. 20/09/19

Haarhoff, J. 2019. First line ammo. Facebook correspondence GRENSOORLOG/ BORDER WAR 1966-1989. 12/11/19

Hattingh, D. 2019. Cover photo context. Facebook correspondence GRENSOORLOG/ BORDER WAR 1966-1989. 04/10/19

Joubert, K. 2019. Former ARMSCOR Senior Manager in the Acquisituib Department. Number of Buffels sold internationally. Telephone interview. 23/10/19

Joubert, K. 2019. Former ARMSCOR Senior Manager in the Acquisituib Department. Buffels history and technical details. Email correspondence. 02/11/19

Myburgh, A. 2019. Operation Sceptic 1980. Facebook correspondence. 01/10/19

Savides A. 2019. Brig Gen (retd) – 61 Base Workshop. Private Facebook correspondence. 04/10/19

Swanepoel, D. 2019. Buffel operation doctrine. Facebook correspondence GRENSOORLOG/ BORDER WAR 1966-1989. 20/09/19

Van der Linde, S. 2019. Buffel operation doctrine. Facebook correspondence GRENSOORLOG/ BORDER WAR 1966-1989. 20/09/19

van der Merwe, C. 2019. First 19 Buffels. Facebook correspondence GRENSOORLOG/ BORDER WAR 1966-1989. 04/10/19

Widd, P. 2019. Buffel operation doctrine. Facebook correspondence GRENSOORLOG/ BORDER WAR 1966-1989. 20/09/19

Ratel

Savides A. 2016. Brig Gen (retd) – Ratel development, history and application. Private Facebook correspondence. 05/11/16

G6

Du Rand, F. 2020. G6-SPAAM. Whatsapp correspondence with project director. 21/06/20

Heitman, H. 2020. G6-SPAAM. Facebook correspondence South African Defence Industry & Military Related. 21/06/20

Potgieter, S. 2020. G6 Rhino Self-Propelled Howitzer-Vehicle. Programme manager at ARMSCOR. Facebook correspondence South African Defence Industry & Military Related. 31/03/20

SANDF personnel. 2017. G6-45 [personal interview and vehicle inspection]. School of Artillery Klipdrift Military Base, Potchefstroom. 27/04/17

Van Heerden, A. 2020. G6-SPAAM. Whatsapp correspondence with project director. 20/06/20

Bateleur

De Jager, A. 2018. Bateleur FV2.. Private Facebook correspondence. 11/11/18

De Villiers, D, J. 2018. Col (retd) SM MMM, SSO R&D SA Army Artillery Fmn & MG Nam. Bateleur. E-mail correspondence. 03/12/18

Heyneke, D. 2018. Bateleur FV2 project team member and instructor on the Visarend. Private Facebook correspondence. 16/11/18

SANDF personnel. 2017. Bateleur FV2 [personal interview and vehicle inspection]. School of Artillery Klipdrift Military Base, Potchefstroom. 25/04/17

SANDF personnel. 2018. Bateleur FV2 [personal interview and vehicle inspection]. African Aerospace and Defence 2018, Waterkloof Air Force Base, Pretoria. 21/09/18

Olifant Mk1A

Carroll, S. 2017. Interview staff member at SA Armour Museum. 02/10/17

Erasmus, R. 2017. Interview Chairman of SA Armour Museum. 02/10/17

Retief, A. 2017. Interview General Officer Commanding SA Army Armour Formation. SA Armour Museum. 27/10/17

Olifant Mk1B

Carroll, S. 2017. Interview staff member at SA Armour Museum. 03/10/17

Erasmus, R. 2017. Interview Chairman of SA Armour Museum. 03/10/17

Erasmus, R. 2017. Telephone interview with Olifant Mk1B project leader. 21/11/17

Harmse, K. 2017. Interview military author. 16/11/17

Olifant Mk2

Carroll, S. 2017. Interview staff member at SA Armour Museum. 02/10/17

Erasmus, R. 2017. Interview Chairman of SA Armour Museum. 02/10/17

TTD

Harmse, K. 2019. South African tank gun designations. Private Facebook correspondence. 6/03/19

Klopper, C. 2019. SO1 R&D SA Army Armour Formation. Email correspondence. 20/02/19

Malan, D. 2019. ARMSCOR. Email correspondence. 20/02/19

Savides A. 2019. Brig Gen (retd) – TTD company acronyms. Private Facebook correspondence. 05/03/19

Rooikat

Erasmus, R. 2017. Interview Chairman of SA Armour Museum. 02/10/17

Hohls, R.R. 2017. Interview former Chair of SA Armour Museum. 02/10/17

Gardner, D. 2018. Former Director OMC Engineering. Rooikat history. Private Facebook correspondence 25/01/18

Ihlenfeldt, C. 2018. Interview with a member of SA Army School of Armour. 11/01/18

Rossouw, D. 2020. Rooikat PPM. Private Facebook correspondence 20/03/20

September. D. 2017. Interview with member of SA Army School of Armour. 02/10/17

Shipway, S.P. 2017. Interview with member of SA Army School of Armour. 02/10/17

Swart, H.J.B. 2018. Rooikat project manager 2001. Telephone interview. 11/01/18

Mamba

De Villiers, A. 2019. Telephone interview. Former engineer at Sandock Austral Engineering: Mamba develop and production. 02/12/19

Gardner, D. 2019. Former Director OMC Engineering. Telephone interview. Former Director OMC Engineering: Mamba develop and production. 25/11/19

Mabulani. 2018. Interview with 21 SAI Battalion member at the African Aerospace and Defence 2018. 21/09/18

Potgieter, M. 2019. Telephone interview. Former ARMSCOR project manager: Mamba Mk3. 04/12/19

Sishuba. 2018. Interview with 21 SAI Battalion member at the African Aerospace and Defence 2018. 21/09/18

Badger

Smit, A. 2018. Interview with Badger project manager. 09/02/18

About the Author

Dr. Dewald Venter is a South African author who earned his PhD from the University of the North West, South Africa. He is an internationally published academic researcher on military heritage tourism. As a military author he specialises in South African military vehicles with a focus on armoured vehicles. He is a member of the SA Armour Museum council tasked with preserving South African armour heritage. This is his first instalment for Helion's @ War series.